annie urrutia

TRUE CRIME

Bad
KIDS

South African youngsters who rob and kill

CHRIS
KARSTEN

Human & Rousseau
Cape Town Pretoria

Published in 2007 by Human & Rousseau,
a division of NB Publishers,
40 Heerengracht, Cape Town

English translation by Herman Fourie
Managing editor: Linette Viljoen
Text editor: Terence Burke
Cover photograph: iStockphoto
Cover design: Laura Oliver, Out of the Blue
Text design concept: Flame, Cape Town
Text designer: Tracey Fraser, PHRASEworks
Set in 11 on 13 pt Corporate A
Printed by Paarl Print, Oosterland Street, Paarl, South Africa

ISBN-10: 0-7981-4901-9
ISBN-13: 978-0-7981-4901-3

Contents

The 'wicked little witch'

Henry McCreadie (29) was mystified: his fiancée had simply disappeared.

Dawn was still in bed when he left for work on Sunday morning, but on Sunday night when he returned she was gone. He had looked for her all evening but had found no trace of her anywhere.

It was very strange – a bank clerk and mother of a teenager did not simply disappear. Henry found something else that Sunday evening that was odd: Dawn's sheets were hanging on the washing line in the back yard, near the flowerbed.

However, Angelique said her mother had asked her to wash them because Henry's puppy, the three-legged one, had been sick on the bed. It was the puppy that Angelique had swung around by one of its legs in one of her moods, injuring it so badly that the vet had had to amputate the leg.

A cup of cold tea stood on Dawn's bedside table.

Late that night, troubled and dispirited from searching for her, Henry finally went to bed. Elsewhere in the house, he heard the subdued voices of Angelique and Lawrence, her new boyfriend. The two youngsters had looked concerned when Henry arrived home. However, one never knew where one stood with Angelique. She was so unpredictable.

Dawn had told him about her violent quarrel with Angelique on Saturday: about Lawrence sleeping over. However, Henry kept his nose out of all mother-and-daughter business, especially because of Angelique's sulkiness.

There was another constant bone of contention between mother and daughter: Angelique's Gothic look when she shed her school uniform in the afternoons and over weekends. In addition to the black outfit with its long black overcoat, she painted her fingernails black and, worst of all, wore black lipstick against her deathly pale face. And she was only 16.

Dawn had already burnt some of Angelique's books, weird books on witchcraft. That had also led to a violent row.

Henry merely shook his head over Angelique's appearance and said nothing. A security guard had better refrain from making

A security guard had better refrain from making remarks about his fiancée's daughter who dresses like some wicked little witch.

remarks about his fiancée's daughter who dresses like some wicked little witch.

On Monday morning when Henry got up, the children were already gone. He assumed they had left for school.

He walked through the silent house and left by the back door. The sheets on the washing line again caught his eye, as did the flowerbed along the low garden wall. He wondered whether Dawn had worked in the garden on the day of her disappearance – on the Sunday. However, the flowerbed did not look like her handiwork. It seemed messy and it was clearly not a cat's doing, as Angelique had replied when he had asked her about it.

Henry drove to Cape Town High School, where Angelique and Lawrence were pupils. He wanted to ask them about the flowerbed. Perhaps he would find a clue in the flowerbed about Dawn. However, the two were not at school. Henry returned to 22 Farnworth Street in Rugby.

He paced through the house once more and in the broad daylight, he noticed damp patches on a carpet. It seemed as if the carpet had been scrubbed to remove stains. He went to Angelique's room, her sanctum where no-one but Lawrence was allowed. Her dressing table was black. Squat black candles, incense and other curious objects were arranged on it. The table resembled some kind of altar. Tentatively he opened a cupboard and noticed the black clothing inside. He also saw black plastic bags, which he felt and then opened. They were filled with soil.

Henry was more puzzled than ever.

He returned to the flowerbed in the backyard shortly before eleven that Monday morning, 21 September 1992. It seemed as if the flowers had been stuck into a pile of disturbed earth, clumsily and hurriedly. Dawn did not tend her flowers that way.

He began to dig and turned up her body.

> **It seemed as if the flowers had been stuck into a pile of disturbed earth, clumsily and hurriedly. Dawn did not tend her flowers that way.**

The satanic murder

Members of the police occult unit were called to the house in Rugby, together with murder and robbery detectives and forensic experts. They also asked for assistance from the Reverend Dawie Pypers, a Childline adviser who was closely involved with the phenomenon of Satanism in the Western Cape.

Apart from dried blood on her wrists, there was no sign of anything unusual about Dawn's body. It had been buried face down in the shallow grave in the flowerbed. She was wrapped in a green blanket and still wore the same nightdress as on the previous morning when Henry had said goodbye to her on his way to work.

Die Burger

Dawn Orsö

Her hands and feet were tied with pantihose.

When they removed the black bag from her head, they saw the wounds. Her skull had been crushed and she had been brutally strangled. The blood on her wrists came from cuts. Her hair was damp and it seemed as if her head had been submerged in water.

Professor Deon Knobel, a pathologist from the University of Cape Town, performed the autopsy. Never during an autopsy of a head injury had he seen such badly damaged subcutaneous tissue as that on Dawn Orsö's head. The blows had bruised it so badly that the tissue fat had turned to oil.

His finding was that she had probably suffocated due to the application of severe force to her neck. There were lacerations to the pharyngeal mucosa. Although Dawn had choked on her blood, she might have been alive at the time of burial.

Prof. Knobel noticed that her dentures were missing.

The murder weapons were soon uncovered: the police found a length of coat hanger rail under Angelique's bed and forensic evidence on a frying pan – hair and human tissue.

They also had two suspects, a girl of sixteen and a boy of seventeen.

A few days after the death of Dawn Orsö, the Southern Cape police arrested two teenagers in Knysna who fitted the description circulated by their Cape Town colleagues. The youngsters in question called themselves Julian Caddick and Ann McIntyre. Their identities were soon established. Colonel Leonard Knipe and Major Peter Lister of the Cape Town murder and robbery unit went to fetch them.

In the back of the police car that took them back to Cape Town, Angelique and Lawrence giggled and cuddled so brazenly that Col Knipe had to admonish them. As with other naughty children, he ordered them to their separate corners.

The gaiety did not last long. A tired and tense Angelique Orsö and Lawrence van Blerk appeared in the juvenile court on Thursday, 24 September 1992, for the murder of Joan Dawn Orsö (38) of Rugby.

The slight Angelique wore a long black dress, black army overcoat and black boots. Her long black hair was tousled and her nails lacquered black.

She was a mere child when her parents divorced and she wanted to have nothing to do with her father, Ermanio. Because the two

Angelique Orsö

accused were minors, only Angelique's father and Lawrence's guardian, Hennie van der Westhuizen of the Strand, were allowed into court.

Lawrence, the son of a Johannesburg anaesthetist, was also dressed in black. His address was given as 2 Clive Street, Vredehoek in Cape Town.

After their court appearance, they were held in the Parow police cells. On 23 October, Angelique turned seventeen in a police cell.

At their next court appearance, Angelique had replaced her black clothes with a stylish blouse and a dark blue miniskirt. Lawrence wore dark blue trousers and a brown and white check jersey. They were more relaxed and Angelique giggled as they held hands.

They had in the meantime been transferred to the Pollsmoor prison's juvenile division. The court referred them to the Valkenberg hospital for psychiatric observation.

In January 1993, Angelique was released into the care of her grandfather. On 19 February 1993, Lawrence was released into his guardian's care after bail of R500 had been posted.

The sensational satanic murder trial started in the Cape Town Supreme Court in August 1993. Although the media were allowed to report on the case, it took place behind closed doors, as Angelique was a minor. Lawrence was already eighteen.

When Angelique turned eighteen in October, Mr Justice Deneys Williamson opened the trial to the public. Curious onlookers crowded the courtroom to see the two "Satans". They were surprised to find that Angelique looked nothing like a witch. Her long hair had been cut, her eyebrows shaved and replaced by thin pencil lines, and she wore tailored suits.

Advocate Jan van der Merwe Sr represented Lawrence, and his son, Adv. Jannie van der Merwe Jr, represented Angelique.

Broken homes

During their trial, evidence was given about the couple's domestic environment and what had driven them to the brutal murder of Angelique's mother. No-one could fully grasp it but a picture began to emerge of broken parental homes and, more ominously, the role of Satanism.

An uncle testified that Angelique was a gentle and friendly child. Although she came from a broken home where her father had often assaulted her mother, her grandmother had raised her to the age of seven.

> **No-one could fully grasp it but a picture began to emerge of broken parental homes and, more ominously, the role of Satanism.**

From 1986, at ten, she started to withdraw and her schoolwork deteriorated. She also started to wear black clothes. The uncle also discovered that one of Dawn's former boyfriends had molested Angelique.

He said Angelique had had imaginary friends from an early age. There was one in particular called Julian. She had been referred to both a psychologist and a psychiatrist, and she had been put on medication. As her friendship with Lawrence became closer, she frequently called him Julian.

A school friend testified how Angelique had once joked about wanting to eliminate her mother so that she and her friends could move into their house.

The friend also knew about Angelique's interest in witchcraft. She once noticed herbs in a drawer of Angelique's. Angelique apparently used the herbs in love potions. Angelique and Lawrence had met each other about three months before Dawn's death and Angelique was unsure of Lawrence's feelings towards her.

Lawrence related how, at the age of eight, he had seen his doctor father trying to strangle his mother in the kitchen. His father had often beaten him, his brother and their mother, and had sometimes even maltreated the dog.

His parents divorced when he was ten and his mother was granted custody of the children. His father, a Johannesburg anaesthetist at the time, paid maintenance only sporadically. In his last year of primary school, Lawrence's mother placed him in a hostel. From then onwards, he led an unhappy life. He was sent from hostel to hostel and from one parent to the other.

When he stayed with his father and his new stepmother, his father locked him in the study, for instance. When he wanted to use the toilet, he had to ask permission from his stepmother. Among his domestic duties were to wash the dishes and scoop up dog's droppings from the garden. His father gave him a scoop for the droppings as a gift on his fourteenth birthday.

When his mother heard about his father's treatment of him, she asked a social worker to intervene. The latter thought the mother was lying because a professional person, an eminent anaesthetist, would not treat his son in that way.

He eventually returned to his mother, but she sent him to Cape Town where he stayed with an uncle for a time. There, too, the young Lawrence was desperately unhappy. The uncle was constantly drunk and his only topic of conversation was Shakespeare.

He said he was happy for a while after moving into a cottage in Devil's Peak with another relative. From there he moved to a commune, after which a young couple adopted him.

Lawrence said he first noticed Angelique during a school geography outing to Table Mountain. She wore a black coat over her school uniform and struck him as an exotic girl. "She was very strange. At first, she wanted to have little to do with me but after my first visit, her attitude changed drastically. It was almost as if we'd been old friends."

He started visiting Angelique, but whenever he had to go home at night, she wept and begged him to stay. "There was something seriously wrong with her. Something unholy was going on. Things were also getting worse for me. I did not enjoy sex with her. I wanted to show her there were other things that we could share. But she almost had an obsession about sex and used to ask what love was without sex."

Later Angelique admitted that she had on occasion had intercourse sixteen times in one day. She also confessed to Lawrence that she was involved in Satanism, but only for about two weeks. She had abandoned it, she said, because the Satanists had wanted to kill her.

Hennie van der Westhuizen testified how he had taken Lawrence under his wing and that he had contributed to his bail.

The day on which Lawrence was bailed from prison, in worn clothes full of nits, Hennie took him for a haircut. Lawrence had frequent nightmares and Hennie decided to try to reconcile son and parents after Lawrence had phoned his father from the police cells. His father had simply said to him on the phone, "I save people's lives. I don't kill them."

By the time they arrived in Johannesburg, Lawrence was very subdued. He was allowed onto the property only because of a misunderstanding: he was mistaken for a gardener. He knocked at the door and his stepmother opened. She recognised him, said brusquely that they were "busy", and slammed the door in his face. Seconds later, his father appeared and chased him from the property.

Lawrence van Blerk

Lawrence spoke to his father from outside the property through the security fence. A while later his father allowed him inside. They chatted for some ten minutes, upon which he spoke to Hennie too while Lawrence waited in the car.

Dr Van Blerk told Hennie he was "poor", wanted to leave the country and was unable to care for Lawrence. All Hennie's subsequent letters and telephone calls in which he begged Dr Van Blerk for financial assistance to care for his son went unanswered. Hennie testified that Dr Van Blerk often changed his telephone numbers.

Lawrence's mother gave him permission to spend Christmas Day with her and her new husband but told Hennie afterwards that she never wanted to see Lawrence again. Her advice to Hennie was to kick Lawrence out because he was "doomed".

Hennie, however, did not do that. While they waited for the trial to start, he found work for Lawrence at R700 a month with a builder.

Mrs Melinda Smit, Lawrence's probation officer, said the two teenagers had known each other well for only five weeks before the murder. Angelique had been Lawrence's first love but she had previously had sexual relationships.

Lawrence and Angelique had started having sex after three weeks. Lawrence, however, did not find it "very positive".

Dr Chris George, a psychiatrist who examined Lawrence, said Angelique had dominated their relationship with her strong personality and had manipulated Lawrence. His own suppressed feelings had started to well up and had exploded against Dawn. Lawrence gained the impression that there was something evil in the house and that an evil spirit had possessed him. He lost voluntary control of his actions.

Lawrence himself testified that his "good little witch" could be a bit sadistic at times. Before having sex, she sometimes sharpened her nails

13

and scratched his back until it ran with blood. "It felt as if there were a diabolical atmosphere in the house. My whole body shook and my heart raced. I could not understand what was happening," he testified and started to cry in court.

It shocked him when he first heard of Angelique's involvement in Satanism. "She said she was mixing a love potion and that she was a good witch who did not worship Satan. But she was still deeply opposed to religion and to God."

Adv. Van der Merwe Jr put it to Lawrence in court that Angelique firmly believed that a "bad witch", one Louise Martincich, had driven her to murder her mother. "It felt to her as if another spirit were entering her body. She did not want to kill her mother. Angelique believes it is possible for people to let their spirits enter astrally into another person's body."

'I fear my sister witch'

Lawrence's version of the murder emerged from his statement to the police, his own evidence and from a police video in which he pointed out scenes in and around the house.

On the Saturday morning before the murder, he had wanted to take his suitcase and leave the house in Rugby. He could not tolerate Angelique's witchcraft stories any longer. However, she wept and pleaded with him to stay.

That night Angelique and Dawn became involved in a heavy argument. He had never heard such a quarrel. Dawn accused her daughter of whoring, among other things, and Angelique wept and shook with rage.

On Sunday morning, she woke him and said, "If I don't kill her today, I'll never do it."

She fetched a heavy frying pan from the kitchen and brought a coat hanger rail.

Lawrence sat shivering on the bed, unsure of what was going to happen. "It felt as if my brains were gone, as if I couldn't think . . ."

They crept to Dawn's bedroom. From the doorway, they looked at the sleeping woman. Angelique turned her head towards him. "Her eyes were glowing red, full of hatred and intense evil. A strange feeling came over me. It felt as if a demon was leaving her eyes and entering my body . . ."

> "It felt as if my brains were gone, as if I couldn't think . . ."

14

They walked to Dawn's bed. Once more they hesitated and then attacked her, Angelique with the frying pan and Lawrence with the rail. "I had no control over what I was doing . . ."

Angelique hit her mother over the head with the pan.

Lawrence squatted over Dawn on the bed, his knees on either side of her body. Dawn opened her eyes. "I saw a surprised and wounded expression in her eyes."

She pleaded softly, "Don't do it." She cried out that she loved Angelique.

Angelique kept on hitting her with the frying pan while also pressing a pillow over Dawn's head to silence her. She kept on shouting, "Kill her, kill her!"

Dawn turned her head away and begged them to stop. She promised Lawrence anything he wanted. Dawn called Angelique a daughter of Satan.

Lawrence suddenly felt intense hatred well up in him, "It was as if I knew no mercy."

He forced the rail harder against Dawn's neck and throat. "I could not control myself and all my thoughts were evil. I could not stop, even if I had wanted to . . ."

He pressed the rail against her neck more forcefully. "My head hurt terribly."

Dawn started crying out softly. Angelique hit her repeatedly over the head with the frying pan. There was blood on the pillows, the bedspread, the undersheet, next to the bedside table, on the radio, and on the carpet.

Enraged, Lawrence forced the rail against the helpless woman's neck. "The thing inside me was inflamed by my past. All the bad things that had happened to me all my life were in me . . ."

Dawn groaned and lost consciousness.

Lawrence put both knees on the rail to increase the pressure on her neck and bounced up and down on the rail. Then he stood up and jumped with his feet on the rail. Angelique helped him. She held one end of the rail and with Lawrence at the other end they forced the rail down on Dawn's neck and throat.

Lawrence climbed off the bed and Angelique felt her mother's pulse and heartbeat. She fetched three knives from the kitchen and started to slash Dawn's wrists. There was more blood but the heartbeat persisted. Angelique went to run a bath.

They dragged Dawn from the bed to the bath and tried to drown her.

Next, they wound a black bag around Dawn's head. Lawrence tied her hands and feet with pantihose and they wrapped her in a green blanket.

Angelique started to wipe up the blood in the room and lit incense to mask the smell.

Lawrence went outside, pulled plants from the flowerbed and dug a hole. "I dug the hole in record time. The evil force was strong in me . . ."

He found a wheelbarrow, loaded Dawn into it and wheeled her to the hole. They tossed her in face first, covered her with soil and stuck the plants back in. The surplus soil they hid in Angelique's wardrobe in black bags.

They tidied up the room, washed the bloodstains from the carpet, washed the sheets and made Dawn a cup of tea.

With their bloodstained clothes and other bedding in a bag, they took a bus into town where they dumped the bag. Later they returned to Rugby, rang the doorbell and waited so that the neighbours could see them come home.

On Monday morning soon after six, while Henry was still asleep, they rode into town again. There they did some shopping, saw a movie and boarded a bus for Knysna.

Angelique testified that after they had cleaned the house and thrown her mother's dentures down a drain, Lawrence had asked her to marry him. She was sixteen at the time and he was seventeen. She said they had thrown the dentures away as it would bring them "bad luck".

Questioned by an assessor, Advocate Rosa Scalabrino, Angelique admitted that she was a "witch" and had read about 35 books on witchcraft. Her witch name was Tavait.

She recounted how her conscience had troubled her for years because she had not sung a hymn for her grandmother shortly before her death. Her grandmother had cared for her when she was small.

"I never wanted to kill my mother, although I got very angry with her. It felt to me [that Sunday morning] as if something supernatural was influencing me, something I could not stop.

"That Sunday morning I still brought my mother breakfast in bed.

"Then things got hazy. It was as if things were happening at a distance, as if I were in a dream."

Shortly after her and Lawrence's arrest, she had a "feeling" that her "witch sister", Louise Martincich, "was involved or had something to do with it [the murder]".

"I was scared of her. I believe it is because of her influence that I am standing here today. I believe she used demonic powers to make me do what she wanted."

She said that she and Louise had mingled their blood some time before the murder.

"True witches are not against Christians. They respect other people's religions. However, she [Louise] had feelings of hatred against Christians. She also told me about rituals on Signal Hill."

Angelique testified that occultists used various mechanisms to gain control over someone. One was the "walk-in" method in which one person's spirit entered another and forced that person to do things.

In a letter she wrote to Lawrence from prison, she talked about her "astral feelings" and explained them to him. When she travelled astrally, her soul moved outside her body. In prison, before the trial, she had paid an astral visit to her murdered mother. She wrote that her mother was wandering "on the astral" at night and had contacted her (Angelique).

"She [her mother] had not yet reincarnated. All I have to do now is to convince her to do a walk-in."

She wrote to Lawrence that the gods had chosen the two of them to murder her mother and to "help her out of a senseless life". The gods were putting her and Lawrence through a "separation trial".

She wrote, "Once they see that we have truly survived it, they will help us out of this mess [the murder case] and reward us for our courage. All the sh . . . we have eaten from these pigs [the police], all the questioning we have endured, and we have not really done anything wrong."

Eyes like a cat

Captain Ingrid Orson, a medical nurse at Pollsmoor, testified about Angelique's demeanour after her admission to the prison hospital in December, about three months after the murder.

"She was very confused. She did not know where she was. Sweat simply poured off her. She clung to me and screamed so much that we took her into the courtyard. I was shocked and started to pray aloud. That was all I could do for her.

"She spoke in tongues and her eyes were rigid in her head, like those of a cat."

Dr David Ruttenberg, district surgeon at Conradie Hospital, testified that he had been summoned to the Parow police cells where Angelique had had an "attack" before her transfer to Pollsmoor.

She was wild and unkempt and they took her to the hospital. "Without wanting

> **"She spoke in tongues and her eyes were rigid in her head, like those of a cat."**

to sound melodramatic: there was something about her eyes. Her face had an intense expression, especially her eyes. It was as if they were on fire. The pupils bored right through one."

Dr Richard Oxtoby, a clinical psychologist and senior lecturer at the University of Cape Town, testified that it was possibly not the real Angelique Orsö sitting in the dock but one of her subpersonalities.

He said she experienced episodes of "dissociative states of consciousness", similar to those of people with split personalities.

He said he was convinced that she was under the influence of some superior power such as a real demon or a force that had arisen from the maelstrom of emotions within her.

He suspected that Angelique's relationship with Louise, the sister witch, had led to her dissociative state and her mother's death. "Angelique is a very intelligent young woman. Her choice of (murder) weapons indicates that she had not acted in accordance with her intellectual capabilities. It is significant that she specifically chose a frying pan from the kitchen with which to murder her mother. A pan from a kitchen belonged to her mother's sphere of influence."

He believed the attack on her mother was an expression of complex interior turmoil.

Dr Oxtoby wanted to hypnotise Angelique to distinguish her other personalities but Angelique had refused. He said he had interviewed her for seven hours and she had changed into another person before his eyes.

An uncle of Angelique's who was a company director, part-time counsellor to terminally ill patients, and advisor to the Western Cape child-counselling centre Safeline, also testified about Angelique's involvement in Satanism. He was a Christian and Satanism did not frighten him.

He said Angelique and Louise Martincich were "blood sisters". He knew that Angelique and Louise had sometimes gone to the beach at Milnerton to make satanic drawings in the sand.

Concerning Angelique's "astral displacement", he said he had once seen her make a key fly from a keyhole and hit a wall while she was a metre away from the key. Angelique maintained that after the death of her beloved grandmother she had spoken to her.

Dawn also appeared to Angelique in a dream about three days after the murder and said to her that she loved her and had forgiven her. That had brought peace to Angelique.

"I don't think young folk realise what they are exposing themselves to when they start playing with witchcraft and Satanism."

The attractive 21-year-old Louise Martincich, Angelique's "blood sister" or "sister witch", testified after she had read everything that had been said about her.

Louise did not want to take the oath (swearing before God to tell the truth) but promised to tell the truth. She denied involvement in witchcraft or Satanism, or ever having been Angelique's blood sister. She testified that Angelique had told her of wanting to kill her mother with snake venom but that she (Louise) had nothing to do with the murder. She denied all allegations against her as well as her alleged influence over Angelique.

> **"I don't think young folk realise what they are exposing themselves to when they start playing with witchcraft and Satanism."**

She also denied that she had gone uninvited to Dawn's funeral and had giggled and laughed while the relatives wept bitterly. She was said to have upset the family with remarks such as "How exciting!" and "What fun!"

Louise admitted to having bought the bulky *Buckland's Complete Book of Witchcraft* and reading it in three months. However, she denied knowing what the occult, Satanism, demons or witchcraft was about or what such symbols meant.

She knew only the broken cross. The "satanic signs" on the beach was a dragon that had resembled a snake in the end. She and Angelique had also not cut their fingers with a blade and rubbed their blood together.

Pastor Gerhard Kotzé of the Paarl Christian Centre, an expert due to his practical experience of the occult, testified that he had been approached by schools in Paarl to exorcise demons from schoolchildren. He said prominent people were involved in Satanism.

He also said one way of transferring demons was through sexual contact. According to the "satanic bible", a woman had to use sex as her most powerful weapon for manipulating people. A witch usually had to be an attractive woman who used her sexual allure.

The pastor said the possibility was "almost 100%" that a demon could be transferred through sex, and Angelique had known that. He found both Angelique's sexual appetite for Lawrence as well as the fact that she had started to call him Julian, significant. It was probably the name of the demon which she had sexually transferred to Lawrence.

Although Angelique maintained that she had been involved only in "white sorcery", Pastor Kotzé testified that that was simply a euphemism for the occult. That was how the occult involved children in the forces of darkness.

Later a schoolgirl who was identified only as Miss X testified about shocking satanic rituals and a mug of human blood at the Afrikaans Language Monument in Paarl.

Miss X testified about "peculiar people who can't speak properly" and who lay around fires at the Language Monument. They cut each other's arms, collected the blood in a beer mug and drank it.

She had also seen Louise Martincich there. "Louise bit the inside of her mouth, spat [the blood] into a beer mug and drank from it."

Miss X said that passages from the 'satanic bible' were read aloud during witches' gatherings. They would then start to bite and cut each other and to drink the blood. "It is a kind of brotherhood, to show that we are all equal and that we share each other."

Once a boy had brought his father's dog, slit its throat, drunk the blood and eaten the raw flesh.

Louise had phoned Miss X one day and asked her whether she had already been initiated at the traditional offering at full moon, a ceremony for turning the uninitiated into full Satanists.

Miss X testified about her astral travels. "It feels so unreal. You leave your body and then you can look at yourself. It feels like a dream. I could do it in the middle of the day."

No demons

No, definitely no, said Professor Tuviah Zabow, head of forensic psychiatry at Valkenberg in Cape Town. All the talk of evil spirits and demons and witches and Satans allegedly involved in the murder of Dawn Orsö was sheer nonsense.

During his examination of Angelique and Lawrence, he could find no signs of an "external force" that controlled them. Neither of them suffered from a mental disorder at the time of the murder.

Prof. Zabow testified that all their explanations were merely attempts to "process" their actions. In order to understand occult or satanic behaviour it was necessary to look at the psychological condition called dissociative disturbance. It was characterised by disturbances of the memory and consciousness, and they did not have such disturbances. He believed their emotions had been

> **All the talk of evil spirits and demons and witches and Satans allegedly involved in the murder of Dawn Orsö was sheer nonsense.**

"considerably excited" during the murder but that would rather have been a symptom of anger and fear than the actions of external forces.

He said Angelique was particularly mature for her age, much more so than Lawrence. He could find no symptoms of schizophrenia in her.

Dawn's injuries were extreme and indicated that Lawrence's levels of aggression were high. He experienced strong feelings of rejection from being spurned by his parents.

State Advocate Anthony Stephens also said the pleas by Angelique and Lawrence about demonic possession and of not being in control of themselves were merely excuses for their vicious act. Lawrence had murdered out of anger towards his parents and Angelique out of hatred for her mother, a feeling that had grown over the years.

Advocates Van der Merwe Sr and Jr both said there were many examples of Satanism in the Bible and it was possible that demonic forces had driven the two children. "Possession by demons is a reality not limited to the sphere of superstition."

Judge Williamson rejected Angelique and Lawrence's pleas about being under the influence of demons and sentenced Angelique to eleven years in jail and Lawrence to eight years.

Both cried on hearing the sentence.

Regarding Louise's vehement denial of any involvement in Satanism, the judge quoted Shakespeare, "The lady doth protest too much."

In September 1995, exactly two years after the start of the Satanist murder trial, Mr Justice Deneys Molteno Williamson died of brain cancer. Three years later, Adv. Jan Andries van der Merwe Sr died of a stroke.

Shortly afterwards first Lawrence, who had met a new girlfriend during the trial, and then Angelique were paroled. Angelique became a mother herself.

The 'Boy Band'

It was wooded parkland, not the kind of place in which a family with little children would go walking after dark. It was a hide-out into which burglars could easily disappear with their loot from nearby houses. House-breaking was a big problem in the area. The police even gave talks at schools to warn children. Although the anticrime project was dubbed "Catch the Thieves" the children were warned not to attempt to catch suspects themselves but to be the eyes and ears of the police.

On Monday morning, 3 December 2001, the sun was shining again after the weekend rains and the air was fresh. The man walking in the park had no thoughts of crooks or nocturnal mischief until he saw a body not far from the entrance gate. It was not a vagrant sleeping off a weekend hangover. The walker noticed the injuries on the man's head and the gaping stab wound on the back of a leg. There were signs of blood on his clothes and on the ground but the rain had washed the worst away.

He phoned the police and they dispatched a car from the flying squad. The officers inspected the scene and the body but found few leads. The rain had taken care of any footprints or signs of struggle. There were no murder weapons or documents on the body or near it to help establish the victim's identity.

The police turned up a car radio in the shrubbery, but it was unclear whether it belonged to the man. They photographed the scene before removing the body. A pathologist took fingerprints and performed a forensic autopsy to determine the cause of death. Two lacerations to the head showed that he had been struck with a hard object such as a hammer. Death, however, ensued from a stab in the thigh that had severed a major artery. The thigh muscle was slashed clear to the bone.

The young victim had been dumped alive but he had bled to death.

A sharp point from a paling fence could have caused the thigh wound. Perhaps the man had jumped over the fence with his loot, the stolen car radio, on his way to find cover in the park. A viciously wielded knife could also have caused the wound. Perhaps there had been a quarrel between criminals in the park.

The fingerprints did not match any in the police archives and no-one had reported a young man missing.

Still, he had to be someone's son or brother, perhaps a husband, even the father of a small child. Perhaps a family had been expecting him home for Christmas. But the body remained unclaimed. The police opened an inquest and removed the body of the unknown victim to the state mortuary until the prescribed time had elapsed and he could be cremated.

The court would determine the cause of his death. It would probably be put down to an unnatural cause such as death due to massive blood loss from a leg wound possibly inflicted by falling onto a sharp paling while committing a crime.

In a country where crime was spiralling and where murders were committed every day, the overworked police set the docket aside. The death of an unknown vagrant, a suspected thief, was not a priority.

The nameless body

In the new year, a fourteen-year-old boy started to have nightmares. Something gnawed at him and he became depressed. He thought constantly about the image that he could not banish from his mind: the severely assaulted man left for dead. That was not how Reinard and his elder brother Heinrich (15) had been raised. They were from a good home. The thought also bothered Heinrich and the two brothers discussed the events in the park that night. They tried to suppress the memory of the events but were unable to do so. They wondered what to do next.

Seven months later, in the winter of 2002, the boy could bear it no longer. It was taking over his life. He could not live with his conscience any more.

People suspected that something was troubling Reinard. They recommended a psychologist, who phoned Hein, Reinard's father, to tell him that the boy was contemplating suicide. Hein was deeply shocked and spoke to his two sons.

Heinrich and Reinard unburdened their young minds of the nocturnal events in the park months before. They spoke of the man who had been assaulted and had bled so much. They named the friends who had been there with them.

> **Still, he had to be someone's son or brother, perhaps a husband, even the father of a small child. Perhaps a family had been expecting him home for Christmas.**

Hein von Landsberg realised the seriousness of the children's thought-less deed. He phoned the other parents but they were apathetic and did not want their children to become involved. He decided to handle the matter in the way he had taught his own children to deal with mistakes: admit your mistake and do the right thing.

He spoke to the deputy director of the national prosecuting authority. The police questioned the two brothers and their father encouraged them to make full confessions. A fourteen-year-old friend also confessed. In return for their cooperation and evidence, the three boys were promised indemnity in the event of any prosecutions.

The three confessed to two events on the Saturday night of 1 December and early Sunday morning of 2 December 2001. They confessed about that mindless night in which seven friends of fourteen, fifteen and sixteen first assaulted a man sheltering from the rain under an umbrella and later rained knife stabs and hammer blows on another. They also told about the lifeless body found the next day at the scene of the second attack.

They named their other friends on that December night. Christoff Becker (16), Gert van Schalkwyk (16), Frikkie du Preez (16) and Reinach Tiedt (15) were all learners at top Pretoria schools: the Waterkloof and Garsfontein high schools. Christoff's father, the respected Dr Christo Becker, was the principal of "Klofies". All boys were from wealthy homes.

The director of public prosecutions ordered the murder allegations against four of the seven boys to be investigated: the allegations against Christoff Becker, Gert van Schalkwyk, Frikkie du Preez and Reinach Tiedt.

Superintendent Vincent Harris and Captain Lynn Evans of the police's violent crimes unit had the names of the suspects as well as descriptions of an assault and a murder. However, they had no victim and no evidence. Where was the body?

If the two brothers had not confessed, there would have been no investigation and perhaps a perfect crime would have been committed.

Taking their cue from the descriptions of events on the December night in 2001, Harris and Evans began their search at the police stations around Constantia Park and Moreleta Park, the area in which the alleged events had occurred. There was nothing in the crime registers in the Brooklyn and Garsfontein charge offices, but they listened to tape recordings of police radio conversations.

For 34 days, Harris and Evans searched for a body. "The purpose was to link the four [Christoff, Gert, Frikkie and Reinach] with the murder. We had to prove their involvement. It took a lot of searching to gather all the facts," Harris later said of the hunt.

On 10 October, the unrelenting search of Harris and Evans was finally rewarded when they found an inscription in an old flying squad crime register: *"Monday, 3/12/01, murder, 14:30, cnr Witdoring and Timeball lane [Moreleta Park, Pretoria], pedestrian found body of black man of about 25, wounds to the head and right thigh."*

It coincided with the place of which the Von Landsberg brothers had spoken and the wounds matched the description of the attack. The judicial inquest regarding the nameless body was amended to a murder docket.

On Thursday, 21 August 2003, warrants were issued for the arrest of Christoff, Gert and Frikkie. All three were in matric and writing their record exams. Reinach had since moved to the US but his father promised his voluntary return for the trial.

That same Thursday the prosecutor in the case, George Pieterse, received a call from someone who wanted to buy the four boys' murder docket from him. He arranged to meet the buyer later that day at Café 41 in Groenkloof, and informed the police. On his way to the meeting, three cars tried to force him off the road and a passenger shouted that they wanted the docket. He managed to shake them off after a wild chase.

On Friday, 22 August 2003, the boys were arrested in the Garsfontein police station and they appeared in court immediately. Gert was due to fly to Cape Town on that day with his school's first rugby team for a match

The four friends were well built, attractive, fashionably dressed, intelligent and confident in court.

against Paarl Gimnasium. He was the team's hooker and a provincial rugby union had already made overtures to him. Christoff was scrumhalf for his Garsfontein school. Frikkie was at Waterkloof, as Reinach had been before his departure for the US.

The trial started on 5 July 2004. All four had finished school in the meantime and Reinach was back from the US.

The four friends were well built, attractive, fashionably dressed, intelligent and confident in court. Newspapers mentioned jars of hair gel and designer jeans. They enjoyed star status and were seen as prime products from two top schools. The next day, four elegant young men graced the front page of a newspaper. Frikkie and Reinach were stern in dark jackets. Gert wore a dark blazer and had an arm around the shoulders of Christoff, who sported a blue shirt. All four looked straight at the camera.

Christoff turned up in court once wearing white slacks and shoes. In the corridor during recess, he sang the old 1992 hit *I'm Too Sexy* by the British group Right Said Fred. The lyrics ran: *I'm too sexy for my love / I'm too sexy for my shirt / So sexy it hurts / And I'm too sexy for your party / I'm a model you know what I mean / I shake my little tushy on the catwalk / I'm too sexy for my car / And I'm too sexy for my hat / I'm too sexy for my cat / Poor pussy poor pussy cat / And I'm too sexy for this song.*

Gert van Schalkwyk, Reinach Tiedt, Christoff Becker and Frikkie du Preez

The four were nicknamed the "Boy Band" after other pop groups of good-looking young men such as the Backstreet Boys, Westlife and Boyzone. Their parents as well as many friends and girlfriends supported them in court.

Christoff felt drawn to Hollywood and wanted to become a movie star. He had been admitted to the New York Film Academy for drama studies but that had been put on hold for the duration of the court case. During the drawn-out hearing, he attended two courses in the US.

Gert wanted to become a professional rugby player and hoped to play for the Springboks as hooker one day.

The future seemed bright.

The four denied killing or violently assaulting anyone. They said they had pursued four burglars in Moreleta Park. That was what the police had encouraged in talks at their schools. Yes, they had defended themselves when one of the burglars had attacked Gert. They knew nothing of a murder with knives and a hammer or of an assault on a man under an umbrella in Constantia Park.

It turned into an epic drama that gripped the country from 5 July 2004, when the case officially opened, until 30 January 2007, when sentence was passed. The intrigues both inside and outside the court involving the four young men, designated the Waterkloof Four, were worthy of a Hollywood movie script.

The other characters in this Pretoria regional court drama were Magistrate Len Kotzé presiding over his last case before retirement, State Advocate Johan Kruger and Advocate Jaap Cilliers, SC, for Christoff.

The Waterkloof Four

On Saturday evening, 1 December 2001, seven boys and a girl were driving to a party in two cars.

A fourteen-year-old boy drove his mother's car, a Toyota Tazz. With him in the car were the Von Landsberg brothers Heinrich (15) and Reinard (14), Frikkie du Preez (16) and a young girl.

Christoff Becker drove his father's BMW. Also in the car were Gert van Schalkwyk (16) and Reinach Tiedt (15).

At the party, Christoff had two beers.

Late that night the boys drove to Steelworx, a club in Hatfield. The older boys went inside for a drink while the younger ones waited outside. All had money; there was never a shortage of pocket money. In the club some of the children – the eldest only sixteen – drank alcohol and partied. Steelworx was popular among the younger set. The year-end exams were finished and the summer holidays beckoned.

Heinrich did not do very well in his exams: he failed Grade 10, perhaps a result of his parents' divorce. He was spending the weekend in his father's flat in Woodhill Estate, east of Pretoria. He invited the group for coffee in the flat after the visit to Steelworx. Around midnight the boys looked for a café at which to buy milk. It drizzled lightly.

Near the corner of Gerard Marais and William Nicol streets in Constantia Park, Frikkie du Preez noticed a man sheltering under an umbrella. "Stop!" he said to the fourteen-year-old driver of the Tazz, "There's a kaffir!"

Frikkie jumped from the car. "Where is Bloed Street?" he asked and slapped the man.

They drove off and continued to look for a café. The group came across the BMW of their friends and told them what had happened along the way. Together the two cars drove back to the man under the umbrella. They stopped and the alarmed man tried to flee, but Gert van Schalkwyk, a capable rugby player, tackled him.

Adv. Kruger, "Tackled him as in a rugby match?"

Witness (fourteen years old at the time), "Yes."

Kruger, "How far away were you?"

Witness, "More or less from a try line to a twenty-five-yard line on a rugby field."

Other boys joined in and started to slap and kick the man, who stayed down. Once the fun was over, the two cars drove off, but the BMW pulled away from the Tazz and raced through the streets. Christoff, buzzing with booze and excitement, was at the wheel.

In Witdoring Lane in Moreleta Park, the three boys in the BMW saw someone run into a park. Christoff phoned Heinrich in the Tazz on his cellphone and told him to come and help catch burglars in the park.

Christoff took some steak knives from the boot of the BMW and Reinach had a hammer.

They found a man who was trying to hide from them and they grabbed him.

To Heinrich it looked like a loose scrum in a rugby game. They grappled and kicked and hit.

Frikkie asked, "Do you know Naas Botha?" Then he kicked the man in the face with his Bronx shoe with the steel-reinforced toecap.

Another witness said, "He kicked him as you would place-kick a rugby ball."

Reinach had the hammer and hit the man over the head with it.

Christoff and Gert each held a steak knife and Heinrich saw the two of them stabbing at the victim: his back, head, a shoulder, and a leg.

Heinrich smelt the blood. The smell in his nostrils nauseated him.

They let go of the man.

Christoff threw his knife away in the veld and Gert hid his in a drain-pipe. They walked back to the cars. Back in the BMW, Christoff made a call on his cellphone.

Witness, "He told the police that there was a black man in the veld near his home in Moreleta Park who was shouting and making a noise."

A while later Christoff phoned the police again and complained about a drunken black man sitting with his woman and making a noise.

Reinach said he had lost the hammer. The boys were worried about what had happened and about fingerprints on the knives.

Heinrich and Frikkie returned to search for the knives. The man was bleeding and groaning when they came close. He pleaded with them to help him and to take him to a doctor. Frikkie kicked him again with his steel-capped shoes. They found the hammer near the gate.

The children left for the flat and their coffee. They abandoned their helpless, badly injured victim where he lay. During the night, in pain and with his blood pulsing from the sliced artery into the rain-soaked earth, the man with no name died in the park.

> **During the night, in pain and with his blood pulsing from the sliced artery into the rain-soaked earth, the man with no name died in the park.**

In the flat, Reinach washed the blood from the hammer in the kitchen sink.

The missing knives worried them. Christoff said they should remain silent about what had happened. He promised one of the younger boys R250 for each knife he returned.

That Sunday, the young boy returned to the park to search for the knives. He found the body of the man. He phoned Christoff on his cellphone to tell him that the man appeared to be dead. Christoff asked him to make sure, but the boy was hesitant to approach the body. He pelted it with pebbles from a distance to see if the man would move, but the body remained motionless. He threw a larger stone but still there was no reaction.

Dr Anton van den Bout, orthopaedic surgeon and first witness for the defence, thought that a knife had not inflicted the stab wound to the man's leg. It had to have been something like a sharp paling fence.

Adv. Cilliers implied that the body in question was not that of the man whom the boys had assaulted. There had, in fact, been two victims in the park that night. The body in question was that of a burglar who had been fatally wounded somewhere else, had lost blood along the way and had gone to the park to die, quite coincidentally where the four boys had assaulted a vagrant.

The pathologist testified that the leg wound could have been caused by a knife and that the rain that night had washed away some of the blood.

Christoff was the only one of the Waterkloof Four to testify. He denied that they had assaulted a man (under an umbrella) in Constantia Park that evening.

Regarding the incident in Moreleta Park, he admitted that there had been an incident. His version was that he and Gert had seen three men running across a road to the park with a TV and other electrical goods. Christoff dropped Gert off where the men had scaled a fence. He drove his father's BMW around to the park's entrance gate. He took two steak knives from the boot as a deterrent and handed one to Gert.

They found a suspected burglar who seemed to be hiding. Christoff and Gert ordered the suspect to get up and accompany them to the car so that they could phone the police.

The man walked between Christoff and Gert, each armed with a steak knife. "It was then that the man hit Gert behind the head. I gave him [the man] a blow from behind and Gert turned around and hit him too. The man stumbled forward.

"Then the other guys [Frikkie, Reinach and Heinrich] came along and started to kick the chap."

Christoff admitted that he had also kicked. He said they had kicked the suspected burglar because he was much bigger than they were and they had wanted to keep him down. They wanted to catch the burglars because the police had earlier held a catch-the-burglars presentation at the school in Garsfontein and they had wanted to help.

Adv. Kruger said to Christoff that the purpose of the evening's activities had not been to catch burglars but to assault black people, which Christoff denied.

He said he had not told anyone about the incident because his mother would have "assaulted" him if she had heard that he had been chasing burglars, as that would have been "irresponsible".

Christoff admitted that he had phoned the police after the incident and had lied to them. He had not wanted to drive his father's car to the police station without a licence.

He confirmed that Frikkie had shown them where his steel-capped shoe had been dented from kicking the burglar.

Under interrogation, Christoff admitted that they had discarded the two knives in the park.

Kruger said, "Now you ran away and threw away the knife. Why did you do it?"

Becker: "It was very dark and my mother had taught me from an early age not to run while holding a knife."

Kruger: "You said your mother had taught you not to run while holding knives. Is that why you threw away the knife?"

Becker: "I did not throw away the knife because there was blood on it or anything was wrong with it. I just didn't want to run with the knife."

Kruger: "Your mother must also have taught you not to kick people who were down or to take a car without permission, not so?"

Becker: "That's right."

Supt Harris was convinced that the body that he and Capt Evans had traced in the flying squad crime register was that of the man whom the boys had assaulted. He also showed photographs of the body to the Von Landsberg brothers and they recognised the man.

The Waterkloof Four were often in the newspapers for incidents and alleged incidents away from court. There was the allegation that Christoff had been involved in stoning a minibus taxi in August 2003.

In July 2004, two brothers were viciously assaulted in the Good4Fellas club in Hatfield and one suffered a broken jaw. The police questioned Christoff, Gert and Frikkie, but it appeared that they had not been involved in the fracas.

Early one Sunday morning, 20 March 2005, Christoff was arrested on the corner of Hilda and Prospect streets in Hatfield for drunken driving. His mother, Mariëtte, said her son had been to a twenty-first birthday party the previous evening at a restaurant in Hillbrow in Johannesburg.

Barely out of school, he was already driving his own new Mini Cooper.

Christoff was sentenced to 100 hours' community service at the Huis Hermon old-age home in Pretoria North. He also had to complete a life-skills programme and attend an alcohol safety school at the Department of Social Development.

Ms Sarie Bezuidenhout, catering manager at Huis Hermon, explained that people who had been sentenced were commonly used in the life-skills programme to help prepare fresh vegetables or wash dishes in the kitchen at the home. "The residents are very interested in the people who work there and they like to talk to them."

A few months later, on 2 June 2005 and in the midst of their trial, Christoff and Gert mingled with girls and TV stars in a Hatfield nightclub on a Thursday night. In the VIP lounge of the Recess nightclub, they themselves behaved like stars. The occasion was the SA elimination rounds of the Miss Bikini World Competition. The well-known actors Neil Sandilands and Ivan Zimmerman as well as a member of the pop group Eden were also there.

One of the guests in the VIP area wanted to know why Christoff and Gert were being treated like stars while there was a murder charge pending against them. "This is absurd. They are walking around with an air of being celebrities."

A Unisa professor of criminology said a reason why the trial of the Waterkloof Four had captured the public imagination was that it was like a drama enacted on a public stage.

"The characters and their personalities are colourful and they wear flamboyant costumes. The fate of the four accused is a continuous thread of tension that keeps people interested in the narrative. Their lives are still ahead of them – what is to become of them now?"

She said it also had to be remembered that they were very attractive.

The magistrate

On Tuesday, 14 June 2005, Magistrate Kotzé found all four boys guilty of both events that occurred on that December night: the assault on the man sheltering under the umbrella and the murder of the man in the park. Both victims remained nameless. The four were released on bail of R10 000 but were prohibited from visiting any place of entertainment without the investigating officer's permission. They also had to surrender their passports.

The magistrate had some harsh words for the four young men, "It is clear from their conversations after the attack that they had foreseen the man's death."

He called it a racial murder and described Christoff as an unimpressive witness of breathtaking arrogance who tried to hide behind witticisms.

He called the defence's explanation of a paling fence possibly inflicting the cut to the man's right leg as far-fetched.

Upon their conviction, the initial bravado and arrogance suddenly vanished. The four stood expressionless in the dock and hung their heads one by one. Family members and friends listened to the magistrate with shaking shoulders.

On Saturday, 22 October, a few months after the conviction, Christoff was reportedly given a black eye in a Moreleta Park bar called the Elephant & Friends.

The probationary officers said in their reports on the four:

Reinach Tiedt was not prison material. His dream of studying in the US and playing rugby was shattered when he had to return to South Africa for the court case. He was the youngest of the group and had tried to impress them with his physical strength by getting involved in the crime. Tiedt was (at the time) a personal trainer at a gymnasium and wanted to study biokinetics.

Gert van Schalkwyk wanted to play the hero and arrest a criminal. He had phoned his mother, Surita Stonehouse, and told her they had caught a burglar. She did not consider the incident important. After he had finished with school, the Puma rugby union contracted him. However, they cancelled the contract when they heard of the murder charge against him. Van Schalkwyk was studying law at Unisa (at the time).

Frikkie du Preez had joined in the hitting and kicking to help his mates without thinking of the consequences. The drawn-out court case had made him irritated and bitter. He was studying BCom (marketing) at Pretoria University (at the time) but had failed a few subjects because of the court case and had to repeat them.

Christoff Becker had taken the knives because the park was dark and overgrown. He wanted to catch criminals. He phoned the police but gave a false name and address. He was (at that stage) studying at the Act Studios in Cape Town where he had been selected for a deodorant ad. He had continued with his drama studies in South Africa. The New York Film Academy had received notice of the charges against Christoff and had informed him that he was no longer welcome to study there.

In the meantime, Christoff Becker's father, the school principal, maintained that the father of the two brothers who had spilled the beans was conducting a feud against the Becker family because Heinrich, one of the two brothers, had failed in the year of the murder. Hein von Landsberg denied it. "I have never had a conversation with Dr Becker. They should have come clean. Dr Becker handled the matter incorrectly."

On 30 January 2007, the curtains rose on the next act of the drama.

The morning before sentencing the Waterkloof Four, Magistrate Kotzé received an SMS from his sister, a retired school principal. "Deal with the faults of others as gently as with your own. I pray that you may be strong and merciful," it read.

In a packed courtroom, Magistrate Kotzé sentenced the four boys to twelve years' imprisonment for murder, and to another two months for assault. He ordered the sentences to run concurrently, which meant an effective twelve years in prison for each.

The magistrate, in his last sentencing before retiring, said, "This was a cruel murder committed by four cowards who have thus far shown no remorse."

He said he had considered the fact that they were very young when the crimes were committed and that they could not be expected to behave like adults. There was also peer pressure.

Regarding the race motive he said, "It is difficult for people of one race to love those of another race. This struggle that love wages in man's soul exists not only between different races but also between people of the same race.

"If loving your neighbour is all that difficult, then self-control and tolerance are good substitutes."

Adv. Cilliers immediately asked leave to appeal and Dr Becker said, "The sentence is irrelevant. It will be better in the High Court [on appeal]."

"If loving your neighbour is all that difficult, then self-control and tolerance are good substitutes."

The last act will follow when two High Court judges consider the appeal. If the judges confirm the magistrate's verdict and sentence, the Waterkloof Four will appeal to a full bench of the Appeal Court in Bloemfontein. There was also talk of amnesty during the Soccer World Cup in 2010.

Throughout the protracted case, many heated debates were conducted in the press about the Waterkloof Four.

Lene Potgieter from Moreleta Park wrote:

"I am a Grade 11 learner at the Waterkloof high school and I want to share my Klofie pride with everybody. The Waterkloof Four story recently did not show our school in a good light and that saddens me. This case has nothing to do with the school. It could have happened at any school and now it is called 'typically Waterkloof'. I love my school and will always be a part of what we call the 'Klofie way of life'. There is a man behind the success of our school. He is Dr Christo Becker (our principal), who makes us want to work hard and who supports us."

Marinus Bell of Potchefstroom wrote:

"As a former teacher at the Waterkloof high school I had close links with the young men known as the Waterkloof Four. They are well brought up and have lovely personalities. I think that what happened had more to do with a case of teenage bravado fired up by our present climate of criminality.

"The perception that these are spoilt children of the rich who lack moral values is false. How do we justify the thousands of murders committed by 'unspoilt children of the poor'?"

On Saturday, 18 June 2005, Johann Rossouw argued in his philosophical column "Glasoog" in the Afrikaans daily Beeld (after the four's conviction) under the heading "Waterkloof Four revolt against father vacuum":

"A tool that can help one understand the levels of violence in South Africa is the concept of the pre-individual fund . . . the sum of experiences, insights, knowledge, virtues, values and such like that a community gathers over time, stores in its technical system and delivers from generation to generation.

"In this vein, Afrikaners after 1948, acting under the illusion that the state serves the community, nationalised their pre-individual fund – finally creating a caricature of what an Afrikaner is (and alienating Afrikaners from their pre-individual fund). At the same time, other pre-individual funds were denigrated and destabilised.

"As a patriarchal institution, the state was especially geared to recognising the fathers of the privileged community and disparaging the fathers of the disadvantaged communities. By the mid-70s, the undervaluation and humiliation of the fathers of particularly the black communities had progressed so far that an authority vacuum had arisen in those communities.

". . . in 1976 Black boys rebelled against the super father of the state – and afterwards maintained the rebellion against the authority vacuum that had been left by their own fathers. After 1994, the roles are reversed. A new generation of Afrikaner fathers are now experiencing the denigration emerging from the state.

"The lamentable events concerning the Waterkloof Four took place at this point in the narrative: four young Afrikaners whose community was labouring under symbolic despair tried to vindicate themselves by turning against the weaker side of an Afro-nationalistic statehood.

"A new generation of sons of humiliated fathers are starting to rise against an authority vacuum."

On 22 June 2005, Attie Conradie of Centurion reacted to this point of view:

"It borders on the absurd to interpret the drunken violence of a group of teenage cowards as the tragic consequence of the denigration of the Afrikaners' 'pre-individual fund' since 1994. A whole generation of Afrikaners was raised on a 'fund' in which physical and emotional violence against otherness had to mask our own moral bankruptcy. For many of our people the Waterkloof verdict is a measure of justice for every nameless person who suffered a similar fate long before 1994.

> **"Let this be a clear restatement to every (Afrikaner) African of a centuries-old clause to the social contract: respect each life as if it were your own."**

"Let this be a clear restatement to every (Afrikaner) African of a centuries-old clause to the social contract: respect each life as if it were your own."

Five empty seats

Little Christoph Taljaard was puzzled by all the fuss and excitement that had enticed even his great-grandmother away from Johannesburg for the weekend. He knew his eldest sister could sing well. Angeline loved singing and she had an important role in a concert on Saturday night. All of them, the whole family, were going to attend.

However, Christoph, barely eight, was more interested in the long school holiday that was imminent than in a concert. It was summer and there were exciting days ahead: first his birthday and then Christmas. Although it was still three weeks away, his mother, Sally, had already ordered the ice-cream cake for his birthday. For Christoph a birthday without ice-cream cake was not a proper birthday.

The sixteen-year-old Angeline's excitement about the concert was much greater than that of her little brother.

Love, Life and Laughter was a true fairytale of passionate love gained and lost. In the vintage film, the actress Gracie Fields played the role of the working-class Nellie Gwynn who met Prince Charles of Granau at a masked ball. She stole the prince's heart and he decided to renounce his royal duties and cancel his approaching marriage to the Princess Grapfel. The prince and his Nellie were madly in love. Then a tragedy struck the mythical kingdom when the King of Granau died and presented his successor, Prince Charles, with a terrible choice. Duty called and Prince Charles chose his country and people above his love for Nellie, and he married Princess Grapfel.

Angeline had every reason to look forward to the evening. As the lead, Nellie Gwynn, she was the one who would be abandoned in love, and her whole family would be watching.

Her family would fill almost an entire row. Five seats had already been booked for them in the Vereeniging Civic Theatre: for dad Chris, mother Sally, great-gran Joey, her younger sister Charlene, and little brother Christoph.

Angeline visited a friend on the Friday night before the concert. After they had finished rehearsing, she phoned home to ask permission to spend the night at her friend's house. It was late and her parents agreed.

It was after twelve when Angeline's parents, Chris and Sally Taljaard, switched off the last light and turned in for the night. The thirteen-year-old Charlene was already lost in her dreams. She slept on a mattress on the floor next to Sally's side of the bed. Charlene had to vacate her room so that Grandma Joey could sleep in her bed over the weekend. Little Christoph was also already in bed.

The 37-year-old Chris and the 35-year-old Sally were the last to fall asleep. They thought about the concert and were proud of their daughter's beautiful singing. They were already thinking of a singing career for Angeline.

The couple were at peace and nothing troubled their minds. It was a bit out of the way where they lived at Mooilande but they preferred it like that. They liked the atmosphere of a farm on their smallholding so close to Vereeniging's Three Rivers area. For protection, they had burglar bars in front of the windows and the house had security gates. Chris's 9 mm pistol was never far from his hand.

It was after twelve when Angeline's parents, Chris and Sally Taljaard, switched off the last light and turned in for the night.

The house was quiet and the occupants were fast asleep in the small hours.

But not everyone was sleeping that night at Mooilande and not everyone was looking forward to a merry concert. The house had been under observation from a safe distance from early that evening.

The two observers were like ghosts in the night: young and fleet of foot. They watched the movements inside the house and saw three adults and two children watching TV. Later they saw the older woman go to a room, followed a bit later by the children. Late that night they heard a phone ring. Then the man and the woman switched off the TV and the lights before they retired.

The two spies watched the lights being extinguished one by one until everything was dark.

They waited patiently for sleep to settle over the house and for it to become completely vulnerable.

They had already identified the small bathroom window that was slightly ajar. The bathroom adjoined the bedroom. The window was too narrow for the body of a man, but the two thought they could squeeze through it because they were not men but boys. They were barely fifteen.

'What are you doing here?'

It was a beautiful Highveld summer morning, that Saturday of 28 November 1992. Preparations were underway in the civic theatre. The sets were being arranged for that evening's performance of the musical *Love, Life and Laughter*. It was expected that a large audience from the community – especially parents, relatives and friends – would attend.

Angeline woke up excitedly in the home of her friend's parents. After all, she was going to be the star of the evening.

A telephone rang in the Vereeniging police station. There had been an incident in a house on a smallholding at Mooilande.

The police were familiar with the dark side of the human psyche; it was part of their job. Even murder and robbery detectives believed they had become hardened to man's inborn iniquity. However, they were unprepared for the cold-blooded cruelty in that house – there had been no mercy for the five residents.

Chris Taljaard had turned onto his right side during the night and he had been shot in the left temple. He was murdered first and had been unable to protect his family.

His wife Sally might have woken up but she could also not get out of bed. She was shot in the forehead where she lay next to her husband.

The attackers found the child, the girl of thirteen, on the floor next to the parents' bed. The shots woke her but the murderers pinned her down and held her mouth shut before they gave her the fatal shot. The bullet struck her in the chest. Charlene was in Std 5 (Grade 7) at the Milton primary school in the Vaal Triangle.

The attackers knew the number of people in the house. They had not yet finished.

The shots also woke the elderly woman in Charlene's bedroom. She got out of bed and met the intruders as she emerged from the room into the passage. They shot the 74-year-old Joey Stephens in the face and she died instantly.

The only occupant left alive was eight-year-old Christoph. The child was terrified. He knew that something dreadful was happening. He knew the sound of gunfire. Christoph crept from the room and tried to flee down the passage to the lounge but he also ran into the assailants. They

The only occupant left alive was eight-year-old Christoph. The child was terrified. He knew that something dreadful was happening.

looked each other in the eye for a split second: the attackers and the terrified boy. Then the pistol fired and Christoph felt the jarring impact on his young body before he fell down. Gravely wounded, he heard voices but lay as if dead. Christoph was in Std 1 (Grade 3) at the Suikerbos primary school in Vereeniging.

Police vehicles arrived on the smallholding. Ambulances and paramedics were summoned. Doctors, forensic investigators and police hearses appeared in their wake. Neighbours and relatives gathered. One of the Taljaard children was missing – Angeline's body was not in the house of death. They traced her to the home of her friend. Her phone call late the previous evening had saved her life.

The shocked Angeline was calmed down and consoled. She heard that her brother Christoph was still alive. The bullet had hit his spinal cord. He had been treated and stabilised at the scene before being transported to the spinal unit at the H F Verwoerd Hospital (now the Pretoria Academic Hospital).

The bodies of the children's parents, sister and grandmother were taken to the police mortuary in Vereeniging for forensic examinations.

Although it was visually evident that the victims had probably died of gunshot wounds, the law required comprehensive forensic medical postmortems. Autopsy reports form part of the case documents in a trial and are considered in a judgment.

An autopsy serves to determine whether there are any other injuries apart from the obvious; perhaps internal injuries that can shed more light on the motive or psyche of the suspected murderer, or wounds or injuries that can lead to an aggravated sentence.

By Saturday afternoon, the wheels were in motion for a massive man-hunt for the murderers. Hundreds of policemen from all over the Vaal Triangle and the East Rand were deployed.

Christoph could provide leads. However, the police understood and sympathised with the boy's state: the emotional trauma of the events to his young spirit as well as the physical shock of his serious injuries.

Before leaving in the ambulance, he said he thought he had seen five attackers in the house. All of them were young. He had asked them what they were doing there when they shot him.

In view of his condition, it was decided not to tell Christoph immediately about the death of his parents, sister and great-grandmother.

With Christoph's life hanging by a thread, the police search underway and her whole family wiped out, everyone thought that Angeline would not take part in that evening's school concert. There was not going to be any more *Love, Life and Laughter* for her.

But she was not having any of it – she wanted to go on stage. "My parents would have expected it of me. They would have been proud of me," she said.

But she was not having any of it – she wanted to go on stage. "My parents would have expected it of me. They would have been proud of me," she said.

That evening, hours after the dreadful murders, she sang the lead to a large audience – and to the five empty seats reserved for her family. Many people in the audience were aware of the tragedy barely twenty hours earlier, and there were tears in their eyes when Angeline sang.

Early on Sunday, detectives received a tip-off from the community. At half past eight that morning, they arrested a young man after they had traced him to the Nelsonia smallholdings about eight kilometres from the scene of the murders.

Later that same day they found Sally Taljaard's burnt-out car next to some ruins near the Goeie Hoek station, about 15 kilometres from the house. They surmised that the car had been burnt to destroy possible leads.

In the veld near the wreck of the car, police found items stolen from the Taljaard residence. There were a video recorder and loudspeakers, but Chris Taljaard's 9 mm pistol and other household articles were still missing.

Vanderbijlpark's murder and robbery detectives were also given the name of a boy, Petrus Lalie Mofokeng. They asked the public's assistance in tracking him down. It was thought that he was in the smallholding areas of Mooilande, Nelsonia or Buysselia.

The detectives also looked for other members of the murderous youth gang. Later that week they arrested one more suspect at Tamboekiesfontein near Vereeniging. They also found another name: Samson Twala. Petrus and Samson were both fifteen years old.

The funeral

The news from Pretoria was not encouraging for Angeline; her brother was paralysed and would probably spend the rest of his life in a wheelchair. Some consolation was that the hospital superintendent, Dr M Smal, had described Christoph's condition as stable, which meant that the boy was out of danger.

Later that week there was speculation that Christoph would be able to attend his family's memorial and cremation services. He had been told only on the Tuesday after the murders about the true events in his parents' home and that he and Angeline were orphans.

The cremation took place on the Friday after the murders. It was hoped that Christoph could be brought from Pretoria by ambulance, but the doctors decided that he was still too weak.

On the Thursday before the cremation, a heartbroken Angeline packed up her parents' things, unsure of her future or that of her brother.

"Little Christoph will have to stay in hospital for three or four months," she told a journalist. "He might stay with relatives but no firm decision has been taken about his future.

"I will stay with my mother's best friend and complete my last school year at the same school that I currently attend. Another disruption will be unbearable.

"After that I will work at a singing career for a year. Mother and them always insisted that I sing everywhere."

Angeline said she wanted to know every possible thing about the events she had escaped that fateful night.

"I don't want to say one day that I should, after all, have gone to see the burnt-out car. That is why I also went to identify my parents in the mortuary. I also arranged the cremation after the funeral service myself.

"My mother always asked for her and my father's ashes to be strewn at God's Window in the Lowveld (of Mpumalanga)."

Angeline looked emotionally at the leather armchair from which her mother used to watch TV. "I would like to keep this chair with me forever. It will remind me of my mother."

Commenting about the Saturday night concert in the civic theatre where she had sung the lead, Angeline said, "I dedicated a song to my parents. I sang it only for them. Everyone in the audience was in tears. I decided to be brave for my parents and for my paralysed brother."

On the Friday of the cremation, Angeline sang a special farewell song for her parents and sister.

Two ministers, Paul Bester and Lindsay Hayward, led the memorial service in the Vereeniging Central Methodist Church. Reverend Bester's text came from Ps. 27:1-4. He said, "The Lord is my light and my salvation. When criminals attack me to kill me, then it is they who stumble and fall." He said it was a sad day for Angeline and Christoph but the Lord would be their strength.

Angeline then sang *One Day at a Time* to tears and sobs from the mourners in the packed church.

On Wednesday, 16 December, Christoph's long-awaited ninth birthday finally dawned. It was a day that he had almost not lived to experience.

Angeline arranged a special birthday party for him in the spinal unit of the hospital in Pretoria. She arrived with his beloved ice-cream cake that his mother had ordered for her youngest child shortly before her death, not knowing that she would never enjoy the privilege of congratulating him on his birthday.

> **It was exactly what Angeline had wanted: to let him forget all the dreadful things for one day. Let him forget terror and death, and his disability that appeared to be permanent.**

Despite the recent traumatic events, it was a joyful day for Christoph. It was exactly what Angeline had wanted: to let him forget all the dreadful things for one day. Let him forget terror and death, and his disability that appeared to be permanent.

After tucking into the ice-cream cake, Christoph had another surprise. Wikus Cruywagen, a young magician, arrived to entertain him. Christoph had always wished to have a magician at his party. Again, Angeline with her indomitable spirit had arranged the surprise.

Christoph watched the tricks open-mouthed. He was especially delighted when Wikus drew a live rabbit from a small wooden box and handed the furry bundle to him. Christoph had already become quite adept with his wheelchair and wove among his birthday friends.

Charmaine Hugo, Christoph and Angeline's aunt who now looked after them, said Christoph had had an ice-cream cake at every birthday. She said her sister Sally was renowned for the wonderful children's parties she could arrange. She had been a mother after any child's heart.

Charmaine also said Christoph would have to stay in hospital for approximately another three months before he could move in with them in the Lowveld and become one of her own children. She believed that one day he would get along on crutches and would be able to discard the wheelchair.

Her sons Adrian (10) and Charlie (12) were also at the party and they said to Christoph, "You're not our cousin any longer but our brother."

A week later, Christoph was allowed to spend Christmas with his new family in White River. Angeline went with him.

Charmaine Hugo later said about the first Christmas without the two children's parents, "There was naturally a lot of hurt, but we tried to have a normal celebration. Among his Christmas presents were toys of some of the popular characters in the TV programme *Dinosaurs*."

The plight of the paralysed Christoph Taljaard, sole survivor of the murderous attack on his parental home, moved the entire country. On Friday, 19 February 1993, he visited his old Vereeniging school Suikerbos for the first time since his hospitalisation nearly three months earlier. He was still under medical care in the hospital, but in the meantime a Vereeniging family and children's aid society had collected R23 000 to help ease his life.

Another month elapsed before he returned to school. Upon his discharge from hospital, he moved in with the Hugo family in White River and started school on Monday, 22 March 1992. He was in Std 2 (Grade 4) and being wheelchair-bound was difficult in an ordinary school.

Later he was transferred to the Meerhof school for the handicapped at Hartbeespoort Dam. There he received specialised care and started to devote himself increasingly to disabled sports.

The court cases

The arrest and interrogation of Petrus Lalie Mofokeng revealed that the terrified and wounded Christoph Taljaard had been confused about the number of attackers in his home on that chaotic night. There had not been five but only two: Petrus Mofokeng and Samson Twala.

At an earlier court appearance in the Vereeniging magistrate's court, Prosecutor Retha Pretorius said the two suspects had maintained that someone called Rasta had forced them to break into the Taljaards' house.

Petrus, who had pulled the trigger that night, was charged with four murders and the attempted murder of Christoph. The docket also contained numerous other charges arising from the events, such as theft (of Sally Taljaard's car, household articles and the 9 mm pistol) and malicious damage to property (torching the car).

Petrus appeared in court alone. Samson had disappeared in the meantime and the police were searching for him.

Petrus said that although he had done the shooting, it had been at the instigation of Samson Twala, the "brains" behind the murders.

In April 1994, Petrus was convicted of the murders. The death penalty still applied in South Africa, but he escaped the death sentence as, at seventeen, he was still a minor. However, he was branded a seventeen-year-old mass murderer.

The ruthlessness of the two young murderers emerged in court once more. They had gunned down the family one by one. First there was the steel-construction worker Chris Taljaard, then his wife, Sally, then their daughter Charlene (who also suffered other injuries), then Joey Stephens, and finally Christoph. The bullet had penetrated his chest before it struck his spine.

Petrus received four life sentences for the four murders. He was also sentenced for the other convictions and received a total of 132 years' imprisonment.

Mr Justice John Coetzee said, "I can hardly imagine anything more cold-blooded than shooting innocent and defenceless sleeping people. Mofokeng had seen them that evening watching TV, switching off the lights and going to bed. He must be finally removed from society."

Petrus started his lengthy jail term, but the long arm of the law had not forgotten that night at Mooilande. They did not forget the boy who had given the orders for the murders and they kept looking for Samson Twala.

More than four years after Petrus's sentencing, the long-anticipated news broke: the second murderer had been hunted down. Detectives of the notorious Brixton murder and robbery squad had cornered him near Carletonville on the West Rand.

Samson, by then 22, had dodged the police for seven years. His victim Christoph Taljaard, then sixteen, was still in a wheelchair.

Petrus was taken from prison to testify against his former accomplice.

On Monday, 25 October 1999, in the Vereeniging circuit court, Petrus relived the cold-blooded murders of seven years before.

He said he and Samson had watched the house in Mooilande on the Friday night. They broke into the house at about three o'clock on Saturday morning (after Angeline had called her parents to ask whether she could stay over with a friend).

Petrus said they had decided beforehand to shoot everyone in the house.

After shooting Chris, Sally and Charlene, they met Joey Stephens in the passage. "I killed her too," said Petrus.

Then a boy came out of a room and ran down the passage. "He ran away from me. I followed him and shot him too."

The boy fell down and lay crying.

"Listen how the child is crying. He is lying in the passage. He isn't dead. Go and finish him off," Samson ordered Petrus.

> "Listen how the child is crying. He is lying in the passage. He isn't dead. Go and finish him off."

Petrus walked to the wounded and paralysed Christoph. He cocked the gun but it was empty. He then left the boy right there, he testified.

According to court papers, neighbours had found the wounded Christoph the following morning in his bed.

In his judgment, Mr Justice Eben Jordaan said those were the bloodiest murders he had ever encountered in his career. He found it frightening that Samson Twala and Petrus Mofokeng were mere children when they committed the crimes.

Samson was sentenced to 120 years in prison.

Christoph Taljaard

Christoph, shackled to a wheelchair, had been trying to forget that night for seven years. However, Samson's court case open up old wounds. To spare him reliving the nightmare, he, the sole survivor, never testified.

In the Meerhof school he seemed to have accepted his fate. He was even cheerful, like any normal teenager. He was a star on the sports field. By then he had been a member of the South African junior disabled athletics team four times and he was aiming for inclusion in the South African team to the Sydney Paralympics the following year.

Christoph spoke enthusiastically of his life with his new family, the Hugos of the Lowveld. They treated him like their own child. He also had good fun with his cousin Adrian when he went home every third weekend.

But the tears threatened to well up in his blue eyes whenever he recalled the night that changed his life, or when he spoke of his physical ordeals, or of how much he missed his parents and his sister.

He was deeply disturbed when he heard about Samson's court case. "It is so unexpected. I have been trying to forget it for so long."

He said the police had spared him the trauma by not requiring him to testify in Petrus's 1994 trial. The second time, in 1999, he would have liked to testify. He wanted to look Petrus and Samson in the eye for the first time since that night. "I wanted to look them in the eye the way they had looked me in the eye that night in the passage of our house before they shot me."

Christoph's account

Although he had never testified, because of the trauma and his youth, Christoph remembered everything about the night of the murder. It had been whirling around in his mind, his dreams and his thoughts for seven years.

He related to a journalist his memories of the night when death visited his home.

The shots and cries woke him. He did not know it at the time but his parents and Charlene were already dead in his parents' bedroom. He sat up in bed, terrified. Through the open bedroom door, he saw his great-grandmother walk down the passage past his bedroom. Then he heard the shot that killed her and he heard her fall.

"I remember I was terribly scared. I lay in bed for a long time before I got up."

He crept to the door with his heart pounding. He was only eight years old and alone in a house with murderers. He peeped from his room into the dark house. A light burnt in the TV room.

"I saw Granny Joey lying in the passage. I stepped over her."

Christoph walked down the passage to the TV room and stopped in the door when he saw a young boy. It was Samson, who looked him the eye. Then he saw another boy, Petrus, who turned around suddenly and also looked at Christoph. Petrus had a pistol in his hand. The three boys stood watching one another.

> **He crept to the door with his heart pounding. He was only eight years old and alone in a house with murderers.**

Suddenly Petrus fired the pistol. The bullet struck Christoph in the chest. His legs buckled under him.

"I fell on the floor. I knew I wasn't dead."

Whether he cried, as Petrus had testified, he could not remember. "I remember that I lay still. I was so scared they would see that I was still alive."

He lay for a long time as if dead. He heard them in the house. They started to strip it and they walked in and out.

"Long afterwards I heard a car drive away."

Once the engine noise had faded into the night, the house was deathly silent. There was not a groan or a gasp.

Christoph had no sensation in his legs. He did not know it but the bullet had entered his chest and severed his spinal cord.

He slid painfully on his stomach towards a room. He slid into Charlene's room, where he lost consciousness on the carpet.

When he came to it was morning. He saw the blood on the carpet under him. He could not move. He heard someone working outside under the window and he knew it was Jakob, their gardener.

"I was so thirsty. I called to Jakob from the room. I asked for water."

"He said to me from outside, 'You've got legs . . . you can fetch water yourself.'

"I told him I had been shot.

"He rushed into the house, picked me up and put me onto my sister's bed."

Jakob Radebe saw the blood in the house. He saw Granny Joey in the passage and, terrified, he rushed out to the nearest neighbours.

The police and paramedics found the boy on the bed.

Christoph heard only three days later that everybody else in the house had been killed. He was the sole survivor and he was paralysed.

He said bitterness still overwhelmed him at times. Then he would remember the soothing words of Charmaine, his mother's sister who had adopted him as her own child.

As a small boy, he would wake up at night from a nightmare and call for his parents. Then his Aunt Charmaine was there to comfort him. When his heart felt like breaking, she held him tight and said, "Christoph, there was a special reason why the Lord let you live."

He believed it and he clung to the Lord.

Christoph lifted his shirt and showed the large scar on his chest. "The bullet missed my heart by two centimetres. I was destined to live."

The bullet exited his back on the right and severed his spinal cord.

Christoph said he could not remember what Petrus and Samson looked like. He heard subsequently from the police that they were wearing some of his clothes when they were taken in for questioning shortly after the murders and before Samson's disappearance.

Angeline started her own family in Gauteng. Meanwhile Christoph, in the care of Charmaine Hugo and her family in White River, kept hoping that he would be able to leave his wheelchair and get along on crutches. He was a fighter and he lived for his sports. He was interested in any type of sports in which he could compete in a wheelchair. He especially liked athletics and basketball.

At the Australian junior championships, he won three gold medals – in the shot put, discus and javelin – and a silver medal in the 100 m.

In 2001, aged seventeen, he was named Lowveld sportsman of the year.

However, that terrible night, when his parents were taken from him and he was left paralysed, kept gnawing at him. He had many press cuttings of articles. Some of them praised his courage and perseverance. But he would much rather have gone with his family on a Saturday night in November 1992 to watch his sister sing the lead in *Love, Life and Laughter*.

The dark cloud of depression finally ground down his spirit and on a Wednesday in February 2003, three months after turning 20, he gave up and shot himself.

Eleven years after the murder of his parents, sister and great-grand-mother, the murderers' fifth victim died, ending his long physical and mental suffering.

The burning bed

The couple decided they could not continue in that fashion any longer. They had tried to save the marriage and had hoped for a solution but had finally realised that a parting of the ways had become inevitable.

It would not be easy because there had been so many dreams. However, only the shards remained, the bitter battles and the accusations.

After easing the worst pressure, the couple took a breather. Fine, they thought, everything was out in the open. Everything had been said, the blame apportioned and the hurt doled out. What now, and what was to happen to their child? The child, their little girl, was after all a part of their dreams. How were they to share that dream, the child who shared their genes? How could each of them take a part of the dream along on their separate ways?

Had they had Solomon's wisdom they might have known. But Solomon held no wisdom for these parents. The arguments and accusations flared up anew. Not about the house and the car and the fridge and the cat and the dog that had to be shared. It was about the child. No-one backed down. Each had an emotional claim to their daughter.

The battle was fierce. Reports were commissioned from social workers and the curtains lifted on intimate personal habits and activities of both parents to see who was best suited for custody of the child. It was the law and not Solomon who had the last word in awarding the dream to only one parent.

Perhaps, they thought, it would help to look at the wisdom of King Solomon (970–928 BC) in 1 Kings 3. Perhaps there was still a solution for the child. They read about the two harlots who had approached the king with their problem about a child.

"'Your Majesty,' one woman said, 'this woman and I live in the same house and she was with me when I bore a child.

"'Three days later she also had a child. We were in the house together; there was no one else, just the two of us.

"'One night this woman's little boy died, she smothered it.

"'She then rose at midnight, took away my boy from me while I slept, laid him down with her, and she laid down her dead boy with me.

"'When I rose in the morning to suckle the child, he was dead! When I looked closely at him later that morning, it was not my baby.'

"Then the other woman said, 'No, yours is the boy that died! The living one is mine!'

"So they stood before the king, arguing.

"The king thought about the matter. One was saying, 'The living boy is mine, yours is dead,' and the other, 'No, your boy is dead; the living one is mine.'

"Then the king commanded, 'Bring me a sword!'

"They brought a sword and the king said, 'Cut the living child into two pieces, and give half to each of them.'

"But the mother of the living child then pleaded with the king, because her heart contracted at the lot of her baby, and she said, 'Please, Your Majesty, give the living boy to her, just don't kill him.'

"But the other woman said, 'If I cannot have him, neither will you. Cut him in two!'

"Then the king said, 'Do not kill the child, give him to that woman there, she is the mother!'"

Those were two prostitutes fighting about a child. How much more fiercely would a mother and a father, each tied to their child with emotional and biological bonds, not battle each other?

When they were married, Solly and Amelia had a similar dream about having a baby. She was christened Salomé.

> **When they were married, Solly and Amelia had a similar dream about having a baby. She was christened Salomé.**

However, the marriage was doomed and when Solly and Amelia, after bitter arguments and accusations, decided to go their separate ways, they did not need Solomon's wisdom when it came to Salomé.

Neither of them wanted her.

The family

Cornelia Reese – everyone called her Neeltjie – knew what she was letting herself in for when she tangled with Solly Deyzel. Solly was difficult to please. He was also two-faced. Towards the outside world, and especially towards his mother, he was the good son and husband. At home, behind the closed doors and drawn curtains of the modest dwelling in Quagga Street, he liked the bottle. When Solly was drunk his other, awful side appeared. Ma Annie did not know that side. She was the salt of the earth and that side of her son would have horrified her.

However, to the divorced Neeltjie, Solly's house was a haven. She was tired of a wandering life with the two boys, fourteen-year-old Christiaan (called Chrisjan) and eight-year-old Dewald. Neeltjie had had her fill of men, both good and bad. Her sons were half-brothers; each had a different father. After she and little Dewald's father had gone their separate ways, her good friends the Venters took pity on her and the boys.

Solly Deyzel

For two years, the three of them lived with Chris and Kotie Venter who were both in the police force.

Then she met Solly and she, Chrisjan and Dewald moved into the little house in Pretoria West's Proclamation Hill. With a roof over their heads, Neeltjie imagined that she and her two boys would stop wandering. The house lacked enough bedrooms and beds. Chrisjan and Dewald had to sleep in the lounge, but at least they were a family again, sort of.

Neeltjie soon adapted to Solly's habits and did not mind being referred to as his kept woman. People could gossip and say whatever they wanted. She gave Solly what he needed and in bed there was no holding him back. And Solly gave them a home, sort of.

Neeltjie soon learnt that Solly was beyond redemption. Ever since he had lost his work at the Pretoria municipality, he also did not hold back whenever he opened a bottle of liquor. He had been boarded because of a back problem and his disability pension was meagre. However, there was always something to drink and Neeltjie joined in. If she did not, Solly would kick her out and find somebody else to match him.

Another woman, a former lover, already hovered in the wings and kept on pestering him. She would not have minded taking Neeltjie's place at the bottle and in bed.

At 39, Neeltjie brought home a little something too – not much – from her job at the pawnshop. Then there was Salomé, who also lived with them and who had to pay rent.

Neeltjie Reese

Salomé also had to clean the house and do the laundry. Solly said she could not expect to stay free of charge. Where was the money to come from for all the hungry stomachs and him unable to work? Then they had to consider the thirst.

For that very reason Solly had taken Salomé out of school the year before. She had to start earning money. It was illegal because she was only fifteen, but who was going to mind if Salomé was not seen at school any longer? Who would dare risk the volatile Solly's wrath?

For a girl of sixteen with barely Grade 10 to her name, the prospects of a brilliant career were rather slim. Work was scarce, but Solly forced and threatened her. He suggested a good job where she would be able to meet many people.

At sixteen, Salomé started working as a car guard.

Salomé's spirit was bruised. One moment she had been a child, the next she was earning a living. The important teenage years, the transition from a child to an adult, had passed her by.

> **One moment she had been a child, the next she was earning a living.**

One day she was still a young girl, always cheerful and smiling, and proud to be a drum majorette at her school. The next day she was begging for money looking after cars in sun, wind and rain. The child in her had suddenly gone.

Her mother Amelia was also struggling and did not want her because she had a man again. They had no room in their hearts and home for another man's child.

It was her father Solly who saw other possibilities in Salomé. Solly, who was so pious in the presence of his mother, noticed his daughter blooming at the age of sixteen. The girl's body was filling out and he thought of how she could earn money. He said that men with cars would notice a girl with a body like hers. Men would lust after her and pay for such a body. He, Solly, thought it would be a fine plan if his daughter minded cars and sold her body to men with cars. Then she could bring enough money home to pay for food and liquor and he, Solly, with his bad back, would not have to work at 45.

Neeltjie could continue to contribute her pawnshop money.

Solly, father of the child whom no-one wanted, also saw other possibilities in his budding daughter. His drunken brain conceived something even more despicable: if other men could use her body, why not him? He started molesting his own daughter and regarded it as his right. After all, did he not give her board and lodging, and keep her off the streets? She was not his dream child any longer. She was at best a lodger.

That was the side to Solly that his mother and family never saw.

Whenever his mother visited and enquired about her granddaughter, Solly proudly showed Annie the large photographs in the lounge. In them, Salomé still wore her hair long, the way teenagers liked it. At sixteen, however, Salomé was way beyond an ordinary teen.

Salomé Deyzel

There was even a photograph in a fancy frame of Solly and Salomé together, smiling at the camera. However, the photograph was not a recent one. Salomé no longer laughed so frequently and her hair was short. It was more practical for guarding cars in all weathers and for meeting men.

Miems Nel, Solly's sister, liked to point out the photo of father and daughter. She would say, "Solly really loved this one."

Martin Deyzel, Solly's brother, said, "He cared a lot for Salomé and always tried to protect her."

And Annie Deyzel, Solly's mother, said, "He would do anything for Salomé. I often told him not to spoil her so but he would say, 'But Ma, she's all I've got.'"

The fire

Solly did not like Salomé's new friend, but then he did not like any of her friends. He allowed her no social life. Let the other youngsters enjoy life. Let them party, go to the movies and chat about things that interested teenagers. Salomé had to work and bring in money. Socialising with friends only restricted the time she had for selling her body.

On Friday night, 15 September 2000, Solly and his daughter had a violent row because she had again let her sweetheart, the unwelcome friend, slip into the house and into her room. She had thought her father would not notice. He was already half-pickled and Neeltjie was matching him drink for drink.

And Solly, in full flight, accused her of not performing her domestic duties either.

She said she did not want to work as a car guard; she wanted to be allowed to have friends.

Solly drank and swore, saying he would teach her a lesson. In his drunken state, he fell on top of her. Neeltjie dragged him away and the two of them made their unsteady way to the bedroom.

For a while, the agitated Salomé sat watching TV in the lounge, where Chrisjan and Dewald were getting ready for bed. Although the rows and drinking were familiar to them, it still distressed their young spirits.

Later, Salomé too announced that she was going to bed.

But late that night, in the small hours of Saturday morning, there was sudden pandemonium in the quiet house in Quagga Street.

It was a young girl's cries that woke neighbour Dries Hamer that night. His son of 19, also Dries, and his brother-in-law, Richard Beneke, rushed outside to see the hysterical Salomé trying to tear open the garden gate of her parents' home. She was screaming that the house was on fire. They also saw Chrisjan and Dewald, half asleep and traumatised.

But late that night, in the small hours of Saturday morning, there was sudden pandemonium in the quiet house in Quagga Street.

Chrisjan said he had smelt smoke from the main bedroom and had unsuccessfully tried to open the door.

The neighbours smashed out a window and grabbed a garden hose. They tried to douse the fire but the smoke was so dense that they could see nothing in the bedroom.

All they heard was Neeltjie pleading for help. While she was crying out, they heard another window breaking.

Salomé, Chrisjan and Dewald were taken to the Hamers' house and the police and fire brigade were summoned.

The children told of a breaking window waking them. They also saw someone jump over a garden wall and run away.

Salomé told of threats made earlier to her father by a woman, one of his former lovers.

The police, fire brigade and paramedics discovered a shocking scene in the house. They found Neeltjie first. She was lying on the lounge carpet and was still alive, but the fierce flames had seared her skin and burnt her clothes off her body. She whimpered in agony. The trained paramedics could do little for someone with 100% burns. They tried to make her comfortable, pushed her to the ambulance on a gurney and raced to the Kalafong hospital west of Pretoria.

In the bedroom, there was clearly nothing to be done for Solly. He lay burnt to death on the smouldering bed. A police hearse instead of an ambulance was summoned for him.

Forensic investigators arrived as well as arson experts with sniffer dogs trained to trace the cause of a fire.

The role of a forensic investigator at the scene of a fire is twofold: he has to determine the origin of the fire and then its cause.

Such an investigation typically starts with a general survey of the scene and the fire damage. Some basic rules are observed: a fire burns upwards and sideways and V patterns of scorching and soot against the walls provide leads to its point of origin. Another rule is that flammable material increases the intensity and extent of a fire. Different temperature states can be deduced from the fire debris. A fire needs fuel such as fabric that is easily flammable, and then oxygen. A fire will therefore only spread where there is enough combustible material as well as air currents.

In the smoke-filled room, it was soon evident that the fire had started on the bed in which Solly and Neeltjie were sleeping. The bed and the bodies had been exposed to intense heat.

The fire had also not started gradually, for instance through a smouldering cigarette or even a candle. In that case, Solly and Neeltjie might have stood a chance. They would have smelt the smoke if they had not been sleeping too deeply in their inebriated state.

The fire had started quickly and had soon reached an intense heat. An accelerator, as it was called, had helped it along.

Amid the smoke and stench of the embers in the room, there was the unmistakeable smell of petrol fumes. That was the accelerator.

The investigators also knew that nothing that merely smouldered could ignite petrol. The forensic experts understood that it was fiction for cars in the movies to explode in balls of fire when bullets pierced their fuel tanks, or when a casually flicked cigarette landed in a puddle of petrol.

They knew that although a burning cigarette could reach a temperature of 700°C and the flashpoint of petrol was only 246°C, this meant nothing because it was not the petrol itself that ignited but its fumes encountering oxygen together with an open flame.

It was beyond dispute that they were looking at a murder scene. Petrol had saturated the flammable bedding and an open flame from a match or lighter had lit the petrol fumes.

The police also saw the blood against the broken windowpanes where Neeltjie had made hysterical and futile attempts to escape. And they saw the bedroom door that she had broken down with a last superhuman effort while already seriously burnt. The door seemed to have been locked from the outside to trap Solly and Neeltjie in the burning room.

The arson experts also knew that sometimes a household product such as sugar was mixed with petrol to make it stick to something like a body. That caused more severe burn wounds.

The confession

Solly and Neeltjie's families were informed about the tragedy early on Saturday, while the police were still busy with their investigations in the house. The Venter family, Chris and Kotie, came to collect Chrisjan and Dewald to look after them while the doctors battled in hospital to save the life of their mother Neeltjie.

Salomé left with her unwelcome boyfriend for his mother's home.

Neeltjie's dismayed and concerned relatives arrived at the Kalafong hospital. However, the doctors had little hope for her and they advised the family to send for a dominee to support her in her last moments.

> **Neeltjie whispered the name of the attacker she had seen in the room that night; the one who had poured petrol over her and Solly and set them alight.**

While he stood at her bedside, Neeltjie whispered the name of the attacker she had seen in the room that night; the one who had poured petrol over her and Solly and set them alight.

The dominee prayed for Neeltjie and she died at eight on Saturday morning.

On Saturday afternoon, the mother of Salomé's unwelcome boyfriend returned her to the Quagga Street house. The police and fire brigade were still busy on the scene. In the street outside, neighbours and curious onlookers discussed the dreadful events. They sympathised with Salomé. At the request of journalists, Salomé fetched photographs of her and her father from the house. She apologised and said, "I don't have a photo with my hair as short as it is now."

Then she said goodbye to the woman who had dropped her off. "Thank you, Auntie, for what you've done for me." She broke out in harrowing sobs and some neighbours consoled her.

Later that afternoon she left with the police. She had to make a statement regarding what she and the other children had seen and heard shortly after the fire.

In the street, neighbours and acquaintances spoke softly – out of respect for the deceased – about how hard-working Solly had been.

One described him as a perfectionist, while another called him a difficult customer.

Neighbour Dries Hamer said, "He was a wonderful person at times . . . but everybody had problems with him."

That same afternoon, Salomé was confronted in the charge office with Neeltjie's dying statement to the dominee. The girl then confessed in a written statement to pouring the petrol over her father and his woman and setting the bed alight with a cigarette lighter.

Insp. Claassens, the investigating officer, said Salomé had broken down and confessed everything. She allegedly said that she and her father had clashed earlier on Friday about her household duties and her work as a car guard. They had then made peace, but when she let her boyfriend slip into the house later that night, she decided she was fed-up with her father.

Salomé was taken to a shelter for young people while the childless Venters decided to foster Chrisjan and Dewald.

Little Dewald later told a journalist, "My mother is dead but I love my aunt and uncle very much and I enjoy living with them."

The two boys seemed cheerful, but Kotie Venter said they had been through massive trauma. The Venters arranged psychological counselling for them. Particularly Chrisjan suffered from nightmares and the two slept in the bedroom with the Venters.

"Although we are saddened by Neeltjie's death, we firmly believe that we and the boys are going to be a very happy family. They were like children in our home when they and their mother lived with us for two years," Kotie Venter said.

Salomé appeared in court on the Monday after the murder. At the hearing, which took place behind closed doors due to her status as a minor, she was referred to the Weskoppies mental institution for observation.

Her face was expressionless in court. She wore dark slacks and a black windcheater.

A month later, in October 2000, she appeared in court after her release from Weskoppies. She was charged with murder and arson. Psychologists found her accountable. A psychiatric report from Weskoppies stated that she was competent to follow court proceedings and to contribute meaningfully to her defence.

Her case was postponed to January 2001, and she was released into the custody of a friend of her mother's.

Her grandmother, Annie Deyzel, still maintained that her son Solly had loved Salomé dearly.

In January, the case was postponed again. Salomé was taken up in a place of safety as her mother's friend could no longer care for her.

While in custody, Salomé started coming into her own for the first time since the tragedy. She was elected a leader and her mother, Amelia, said, "My child is blooming and looks very good. She is another person. I don't know her any more."

Salomé also attended a Christian camp and decided to resume school. She enrolled as a learner at the school in the place of safety.

In June 2002, all charges against Salomé were withdrawn in the Pretoria magistrate's court. Despite Neeltjie Reese's deathbed statement about the guilty person and Salomé's own confession, there was insufficient evidence against her.

Minette Wilsenach, senior state prosecutor for the district court, confirmed the withdrawal. However, she added, "The police investigation will continue. If any evidence should emerge that could lead to a conviction, she will be charged again."

According to Heidi Barnard, Salomé's lawyer, it appeared that the state's case was based on Salomé's statement to a policeman without her mother or a lawyer being present. A statement by a child without the presence of a guardian or a lawyer was inadmissible in court. Without such a statement, the state could not prove that Salomé had set the fire which killed Solly and Neeltjie.

She was released from the place of safety and she found work in a restaurant.

In the meantime, the police did not rest. They knew who the guilty party was and they were not going to let her get away with murder. In August 2002, almost two years after the fire, a warrant was issued for Salomé's arrest. By then she was eighteen. Her name could be published for the first time and people could know that she was going to be charged once again with the "petrol bomb" murder of her father.

Prosecutor Lamson Nemakwarani said Salomé's mother maintained that she did not know her daughter's whereabouts. Salomé had packed up her things and disappeared. Amelia, the mother, had married again in the meantime.

On the new charge sheet, Salomé's last address was given as the Salvation Army in Pretoria.

Salomé was finally traced and she appeared in court in Pretoria in October 2002. She said, "I am not the same any more. I used to love singing and I enjoyed nature and the outdoors . . ."

About her youth she said, "We always struggled and we were very poor.

"After my father's death I tried hard to carry on with my life but I carry the strain of the court case with me. My father and I had our differences but there was never any hatred. My relationship with my mother is good."

She said her mother could not be in court with her because she had recently had a neck operation. "She is recovering at home but I know that she and the rest of the family are behind me one hundred percent.

"Many people condemn me without really knowing what happened. I am tired and I just want it all to end. I know the Lord is on my side."

'Where's my mother?'

In January 2003, Salomé again stood trial in the Pretoria regional court. Once again, she was charged with two counts of murder and one of arson.

She admitted guilt to the charges and said she had to sell her body as a prostitute for drinking money for her father, who had previously been declared medically unfit to work.

Advocate Johann Engelbrecht, SC, her legal counsel, said neither of Salomé's parents had wanted her after the break-up of their marriage.

Her father had taken her from school at fifteen and put her to work as car guard so that she could pick up men. The money she made as a prostitute went to her father.

The advocate said Solly Deyzel had also molested Salomé.

"At sixteen she had nowhere to turn. She was very young. On the night of the incident, there had been a quarrel between herself and her father after the visit of a boyfriend.

"Her father probably did not want her to lead a normal social life because it would have interfered with her work as a prostitute."

> **Her father had taken her from school at fifteen and put her to work as car guard so that she could pick up men. The money she made as a prostitute went to her father.**

Adv. Engelbrecht also said in court, "Parents usually fight over who gets custody of the children. But neither wanted her. She had to pay board and lodging to her father and sell her body as a prostitute to pay the rent."

He submitted to the court that Solly and Neeltjie had gone to bed inebriated that Friday night.

Salomé had watched TV and later went outside to the garage. There she had found some petrol in a two-litre cola bottle. In the bedroom, she had poured it over her sleeping father and Neeltjie, and had lit the bed with a cigarette lighter.

In her judgment, in which she found Salomé guilty of all the charges against her, Magistrate Magriet Cook said, "There is no doubt that these facts [about Salomé's distressing circumstances] justify a lesser sentence than the legally prescribed minimum."

The magistrate sentenced Salomé to ten years' imprisonment.

As the weeping Salomé turned around in the dock to find some support and comfort from her mother, there was no sign of Amelia.

"Where is my mother?" Salomé cried, searching for her mother.

She had not seen Amelia turn her back on her and walk away only minutes before sentence was passed.

Later Heidi Barnard, Salomé's lawyer, revealed Amelia's excuse: Salomé was causing marriage problems between Amelia and her new husband.

In January 2004, after having served a year of her sentence in the Johannesburg women's prison, Salomé told how her life had changed in prison.

She also wrote a letter to a women's magazine in which she pleaded for a sponsor to help her obtain her matric in prison.

Frank Lombaard of Marble Hall, a cousin of Solly's, said that as a child she had often stayed on the farm with him and his wife Cornelia during the holidays. "We would like to help her and give her the opportunity to finish her matric."

Bianka Venter (19) of Riviera in Pretoria had been at primary school with Salomé. She remembered her as a friendly little girl. "She always smiled and she was crazy about drum majorettes."

Salomé was detained in a single cell. She wrote poems and sang the songs she heard on a radio. "I am mad about country music. As a child, my mother taught me to play the piano. I would also like to learn to play the guitar.

"One evening I was sitting alone in my cell above the wards for mothers with children. I heard babies crying. Keys were clinking in the silence and steel doors creaked. I could hear piano music in the background.

"At that moment something happened inside me. I decided to carry on with my life, to pass matric and to study towards becoming a child psychologist.

"I particularly want to become a child psychologist in order to help abused children speak up. I always remained silent and bottled everything up. Then I exploded like a bomb.

"Before anyone else explodes I want to tell them that they must speak up. Simply open your mouth and talk.

"You won't be wasting your breath, although it may sometimes feel like that. I felt like that at times. But it is worth talking. It will keep you out of jail."

About that dreadful Friday night of the fire, she said, "That evening my father fell on top of me. He was drunk and I just broke up. I could not take it any longer. But I only wanted to frighten him."

> "Before anyone else explodes I want to tell them that they must speak up. Simply open your mouth and talk."

Once she had served her sentence, she wanted to speak to her father's family, to tell them how sorry she was about what she had done.

"I know he was their child and brother. Perhaps they won't accept my remorse and they will probably never understand it because they always saw only my father's good side."

And she also had dreams, she said . . . she often dreamt about what she was going to do with her life when she left prison, although at that stage there was still no child in her young dreams.

Baby's gang

On Thursday, 7 June 2001, the last member of a Pretoria teenage gang was sent to prison. Five young friends – all mere children and some of them still at school – were to serve sentences totalling 66 years. They were being punished for an insane orgy of lawlessness that lasted sixteen days.

During their spree, the gang carried out six armed robberies before it all suddenly ended after the seventh and failed attempt.

A depressing picture unfolded during the sensational court cases. It was a picture of youngsters abandoning themselves to alcohol and drugs, unbridled sex and finally to crime. It drew attention to the role of dysfunctional family lives and to youthful cries for help that went unheeded.

The five youngsters were far from trashy. They came from affluent homes and attended top schools.

The informal leader of the gang was a pretty and slender girl who captured the country's imagination when she appeared in leg-irons on the front page of a newspaper. Readers wielded their pens and fierce polemics ensued. It even led to political debates about how the problems of the country's youth should be tackled and about the sensitising of parents to recognise danger signals in order to avoid similar tragedies.

Tanya Oosthuizen became somebody about whom movies could be made, especially once it was known that her lover had manipulated her and the gang from behind prison bars to commit the crimes.

The lover

At 22, André Venter knew how easy it was to get money without having to work for it. He was a charismatic young man who loved life. And the girls adored him. He had met the brunette at the beginning of the year. She was barely eighteen and was an escort. She had been in matric the year before.

Tanya was not afraid of joining him on his escapades. He also liked the nickname she had given him: Baby.

However, in July 1999, Baby was in deep trouble. He was sitting in a police cell in Moot in Pretoria facing serious charges of car theft and robbery.

The court had refused him bail and Tanya was on the outside, free to do as she pleased. The police had arrested them after that job in Pretoria North when they robbed the video shop. The police maintained that Baby and Tanya had gone to commit the robbery and that she had waited in her car to make the getaway once he emerged with the money. Both of them, Baby and Tanya, had naturally hotly denied it.

Then she took the oath and was given indemnity. The police released her and she had to testify against him. What Baby had heard, though, was that she had had regrets and that she had wanted to retract her statement. What he heard was that she still loved him and would do anything for him. Baby believed it and instructed her to keep a diary in which she had to note down everything, so that she – on the outside – would not forget all the things that they had said and discussed.

André (Baby) Venter

That Saturday, Baby was looking forward to a special visit from his pretty girl who loved him. It was going to be special because he would be able to leave his cell and chat to Tanya in the charge office, even though he had to wear leg-irons.

They would be able to talk and discuss entries for the diary.

However, after Tanya's visit that Saturday in the Moot police station, things went badly wrong. Baby and a police inspector were alone, there was a bloody struggle and two versions of what had happened: Baby's and that of Inspector Lucas Mthembu. Two more counts were added to the charge sheet against Baby Venter: attempted escape and attempted murder.

> **Baby believed it and instructed her to keep a diary in which she had to note down everything, so that she – on the outside – would not forget all the things that they had said and discussed.**

Baby's version: he had stabbed Insp. Mthembu with a clasp knife with a 23 cm blade because the inspector had hit him over the head with his own leg-irons, allegedly because Baby had refused to compensate the inspector for the privilege of Tanya's "special visit". Baby also said in his defence he was scared the inspector would shoot him. He had simply defended himself with the knife.

63

Insp. Mthembu's version: he had first locked his service pistol in the safe, as prescribed, before going to Baby's cell. He was unarmed while removing Baby's leg-irons. Baby had attacked him with the knife and tried to murder him in an attempt to escape.

Shortly after the incident, police sniffer dogs had found Baby in the ceiling of the police station building.

The investigating officer, Detective Sergeant Rian Schoeman, later said it was a miracle that Insp. Mthembu was still alive. He had seventeen stab wounds and his throat had been partially slit in a cut that stretched from his windpipe to a neck vertebra. "The knife had narrowly missed the main artery."

He also had cuts on his arms and was away from work for almost a year.

The police suspected that Tanya had smuggled the knife in for Baby. Later, when they confiscated her diary, they allegedly found notes on comprehensive escape plans and route references in it.

Insp. Mthembu's wounds and Tanya's evidence in court indicated that Baby Venter was far from being such a "nice and decent boy" as her parents had first thought. Magistrate Kallie Bosch called him a thug and Tanya confessed in court that while she was escorting, Baby had been unemployed and probably involved in car theft. He had also managed and manipulated her life from prison after his arrest.

She and four young people had to rob and steal money so that Baby could afford the best legal counsel to rid him of his problems with the law.

The team

Four young friends used to meet regularly in a sparsely furnished flat in Sunnyside. There they played computer games and chatted about girls and school. All were from good homes but they lacked a solid family life. They sought out each other for company and for sharing confidences.

William was barely sixteen when he and his elder sister Sally (20) were suddenly left to their own devices. Without a parental home, the two siblings moved into the Sunnyside flat where they had to care for themselves. She worked as a waitress and he was a Grade 11 learner at a private school. It was a survival struggle, and even if they occasionally received money from their parents, they never received any love.

Young William Prinsloo's good friend was a schoolmate, Mark Flascas from Garsfontein. The other two members of the quartet were Adriaan van Zyl, who also lived in Sunnyside, and Manuel da Silva from Centurion. Manuel did not have the quickest mind around.

William's sister also introduced him to one of her old school friends from the Pretoria High School for Girls, the pretty Tanya Oosthuizen. Tanya, William was interested to hear, worked as an escort and had been in matric only the year before.

Young William, quite streetwise for his age, knew enough to keep his hands to himself. Tanya had a boyfriend and it was a good idea not to get on the wrong side of André (Baby) Venter.

In any case, the more he saw of Baby, the more William's admiration grew for him. Baby knew how to enjoy life and he always had money, although he did not appear to have a proper job.

Then, in July 1999, William heard that Tanya and Baby had been arrested after they had robbed a video shop. Tanya, however, had been released.

Tanya moved into William and his sister's flat and she met the other members of the gang who regularly came to play computer games.

> **In any case, the more he saw of Baby, the more William's admiration grew for him. Baby knew how to enjoy life and he always had money, although he did not appear to have a proper job.**

The boys thought Tanya had a great body and with Baby in jail . . . but Tanya had other plans. She thought she could put the boys to good use and she did not mind sharing her body. She had done it before, for money, and could do it again to help Baby.

One evening she had a big fright: at a traffic light in Stormvoël Road in Pretoria, three men bashed in her car window and held a gun to her head. They wanted to hijack her car but ran off when an approaching car flashed its lights at them. Determined to protect herself, Tanya bought a firearm for R1 000.

She visited Baby regularly: whenever he could phone her and was allowed to leave his cell as an awaiting-trial prisoner to receive visitors. They spoke about their love and he told her what to jot down in her diary. She also told him about William Prinsloo, Mark Flascas, Adriaan van Zyl and the slow-witted Manuel da Silva.

Not a lot was said about the sex and the Ecstasy and the LSD and the booze, though.

When Tanya visited Baby, she often had a copy of the *Junk Mail* with her. It was quite innocent; the police could search her personal effects all they wanted. People could advertise anything for sale in the *Junk Mail*. People advertised cars, furniture, TV sets, video recorders, sound equipment, even jewellery, when they needed money.

When Tanya visited Baby, they often paged through the *Junk Mail* and marked items and the sellers' names and contact details. That was what prospective buyers did when they were looking for items to buy in the *Junk Mail* and something caught their eye.

Back in the flat, Tanya and William discussed one of the items marked in the *Junk Mail*: Ms Vanessa Jones of Garsfontein wanted to sell her Honda Civic. They hatched a plan.

The raids

The Baby Gang made their first raid on Sunday, 19 March 2000.

William, looking older than his sixteen years, was cocky and self-assured. He phoned Ms Jones. He was interested in the Honda and wanted to examine it. They arranged to meet at a shopping centre in Faerie Glen.

> **When Tanya visited Baby, they often paged through the *Junk Mail* and marked items and the sellers' names and contact details.**

Later that morning, Manuel da Silva turned up at the flat. Tanya was serving apple schnapps and wine, and they took out drugs. Manuel had a car.

William told Manuel they had to help someone. He concocted a story to convince Manuel to be their accomplice: something about an insurance matter and a Honda that had to disappear so that the owner could claim the insurance money to buy an Audi A4.

Manuel, not the sharpest pencil in the box, agreed to drive William and Tanya to their appointment in his car.

Ms Jones was happy to take William and Manuel for a short test run. Tanya and Ms Jones's fiancé stayed behind at the shopping centre where they had a soft drink and chatted before Tanya drove off in Manuel's car.

During the test drive, William suddenly pulled out a pistol and pointed it at the terrified owner. They stopped and she tried to make a call on her cellphone. Manuel, surprised by this new angle to the sale, put a knife to her throat and took away the cellphone. They tied her up, forced her from the Honda and raced away.

Tanya and William sold the Honda, then worth about R92 000, for R3 000. She pocketed half the spoils.

William said after the episode that cars were not worth the effort. Jewellery sounded like more and easier money. More telephone discussions with Baby followed and again they consulted the *Junk Mail*.

Mrs Johanna Riana Malan, a 60-year-old pensioner from Lynnwood Manor, advertised a precious gold pendant set with diamonds. She needed the money for medical expenses. She had designed the pendant herself and it had been valued at R29 000.

Late on Monday night, 20 March, a day after Ms Jones had been robbed of her Honda, Mrs Malan received a phone call from a young woman who was apparently prepared to drive all the way from Johannesburg to view the pendant. The caller asked if it would be convenient and enquired after Mrs Malan's husband.

Mrs Malan was uneasy. She had been divorced for 26 years and she asked a friend, Pieter de Klerk, to come over and pretend to be her husband.

She let Tanya, William and the thin and very nervous Mark Flascas into her home. Tanya did most of the talking. She said she had inherited some money and wanted to spoil herself. In any case, a pendant was a good investment, she said.

Tanya hung the pendant around her neck and looked at herself in a mirror, asking Mrs Malan how it looked on her. That was the sign for William.

For Mrs Malan the subsequent events were like a scene from a movie: William pulled a cocked pistol from one of his boots and pointed it at her and Pieter de Klerk.

Tanya shouted out instructions while looking for more jewellery.

William shouted at Mark to tie up the victims. Mark trembled so severely that he could do nothing and William then had to tie up the two on the floor with a telephone cord.

They fled with Mrs Malan's handbag, the diamond pendant and a twenty-dollar coin set in gold.

The third robbery took place a week later, on Monday, 27 March.

Again, William persuaded the gullible Manuel to go along under the pretence that William's father was looking to buy a laptop computer. There was an advertisement for just such a computer for sale. Manuel had a car in which to take them there. Mark went along because he was knowledgeable about IT technology and they did not want to buy a dud.

Manuel drove to the home of Mr Johann Strey in Windgate Park. Once again, William pulled out the gun. They kicked and hit Mr Strey and his father, and robbed them of a laptop, TV, video recorder and sound system.

William sold the TV for R800 and used the money to fill Manuel's car with petrol. Tanya got the laptop and Mark took the video recorder. Mark then decided that the robberies were getting on his nerves and that he wanted out. He later fled to Cape Town.

On Saturday, 1 April, William and Tanya struck Video Den, belonging to Mr Charles Wilson, in Claremont in Pretoria. Once again armed, they robbed him of video machines, CDs and cash.

The next day, William was all worked up and ready for more. He hijacked the car of Mr Riaan Hefer in New Muckleneuk and later that day rallied an old friend, Adriaan van Zyl, to help him for the first time.

Kind-hearted Mr Brandon Story gave the two friends a lift in Hatfield. Adriaan sat in front with Mr Story, keeping him distracted while William took out the pistol. They forced Story to drive to Erasmia, where they dropped him off and then drove back to Sunnyside in his car.

The next day, Monday, 3 April, things started to go badly wrong for William and Adriaan. They drove Mr Story's car to the house of Mr Brian Alton in Brooklyn and tried to rob him of two watches.

Mr Alton resisted. Two shots were fired, but he overpowered William and Adriaan, and locked them in a walk-in cupboard before phoning the police.

The police questioned them and before long, they had all the names.

The Baby Gang's crime spree had lasted only sixteen days.

The sentences

Mark Flascas (18) was the first of the youngsters to be sentenced. He pleaded guilty to participating in the robberies of the pensioner, Mrs Malan, and of Mr Strey.

He recounted the attack on Mrs Malan, "I trembled like mad and could not tie them up. I wanted to be accepted (by my fellow gangsters) and I did not think rationally."

According to a probation officer, Mark was one of four children from a respectable but strict parental home. He described his father's discipline as aggressive and rigid, with conservative disciplinary methods. He was a loner who left school in 1998 to study at home. It did not work out and he went to Capital College in Pretoria where he met William.

After the Strey robbery, he tried to avoid the gang. Then William called him from prison (after the failed attempt to rob Mr Alton) and told him that the police were looking for him too. Mark fled to Cape Town, where another friend phoned him to say that his parents loved him and would stand by him. He handed himself over to the police in Bellville and patched things up with his parents.

In court, Mark testified that William and Tanya had received telephonic instructions from Baby Venter in prison before every robbery.

On Friday, 7 July 2000, Mark was sent to prison for six years but in 2002 he was paroled.

William Prinsloo turned eighteen while locked up in a cell. He was sentenced the day after Mark and he cursed the day he ever met Tanya.

He pleaded guilty to all six counts of armed robbery and one of attempted robbery, when he and Adriaan tried to steal Mr Alton's two watches and they were overpowered by him.

In William's court case the macabre tale of the five teenagers unfolded. It was a tale of drugs and robberies, and of Tanya who had manipulated the younger William with sex.

An evaluation report described William as a psychopath. However, Magistrate A C Bekker told him in court, "It is tragic for someone with such enormous potential to make himself guilty of such violations. At no stage did the court gain the impression that you were a passive puppet."

An educational psychologist, Ms Antoinette Human, said in her report that William had admired Tanya's boyfriend Baby because he knew how to get hold of money easily.

"After Baby Venter's arrest, William considered it his duty to help Tanya Oosthuizen procure money for Venter's legal representation."

Ms Human said William regularly took Ecstasy and LSD before a robbery. He had personally wanted to handle the firearm – allegedly Tanya's – because he trusted himself with it and there would have been no danger of any shooting.

Ms Human sketched a disturbing picture of William's domestic background: his parents divorced when he was five years old. At thirteen he ran away once and at fifteen he started using drugs. His father did contract work in African countries and was rarely home with his children, William and Sally. William told the psychologist that on the occasions that his father was home his father had maltreated him. His father was also obsessively jealous of his mother.

William's mother had berated her fine-featured son as a homosexual prostitute.

Ms Human said William had regularly clashed with authority structures in the top schools he had attended. He enjoyed humiliating teachers in front of a class. When he was threatened with suspension, his mother went to plead for him. He was finally expelled from a private school after stealing money from the tuck shop.

When his mother remarried and relocated to the US, William attended Capital College as a Grade 11 learner. The sixteen-year-old William and his elder sister then had to fend for themselves in a flat in Sunnyside.

He was in matric when they committed the robberies.

The psychologist said his parents had given him money but had not taught him respect for other people.

On Monday, 10 July 2000, William was sentenced to 24 years in prison.

In 2004, his father visited him in prison and they were reconciled. William remarked, "For the first time I could talk to my father about personal matters."

William was completing matric at the time, after which he wanted to tackle a BCom degree in prison.

Adriaan van Zyl (18) participated in the last two robberies upon William's instigation. Adriaan saw his role as that of protector: he had to see to it that his "best friend" William came to no harm. Such acceptance and recognition were important to Adriaan.

Adriaan's parents were divorced when he was five years old. He, too, had had a poor relationship with his father. Although his mother had loved him, she had worked hard and did not have much time. A report submitted to the court stated that his sister had raised him.

In high school, he socialised with the wrong friends and left school after failing Grade 11.

His legal representative said Adriaan was guilty only because people with criminal intent had influenced him.

Magistrate R de Vos said he had considered Adriaan's youth but it was clear that most violent crimes were committed by youths younger than 21. "You relied on the good nature of your victims," he said to Adriaan.

On Friday, 1 September 2000, he sentenced Adriaan to fifteen years' imprisonment. Although Adriaan's legal team described the sentence as "shockingly inappropriate", his appeal was rejected.

A court report described Manuel da Silva (19) as mentally retarded.

He admitted guilt on the counts of armed robbery of Ms Jones and Mr Strey.

Manuel left school after twice failing Grade 8. The report said that 97% of people in his age group were more intelligent than he was.

His father, a hard-working restaurant owner, was emotionally absent and uninvolved with his son.

His mother was a housewife and she, on the other hand, was enormously overprotective and had spoiled her son. She refused that Manuel be sent to a special school, believing that he would get by with extra lessons.

Even in primary school, he could not adapt and had to have regular psychological counselling. Manuel could not deal with conflict and passively allowed his friends to manipulate him.

He worked in a café on weekends. He saved money and bought a car in which he drove his friends around to gain acceptance.

In a report to the court, Manuel said his friend William was a hero to him and he looked up to him. He had also used dagga and harder drugs with William, who had told him about a plan to make money for Tanya's boyfriend in prison.

Manuel's legal representative, Mr Wessie Wessels, said in court that William and Tanya had often plied Manuel with liquor and drugs, and had exploited him because he was "naïve and dumb".

After participating in two robberies into which he had been conned, Manuel had told William and Tanya that they were "barbaric".

On Thursday, 7 June 2001, almost a year after William and Mark were jailed, Manuel was sentenced to eight years in prison.

Magistrate W W P Moyses told Manuel, "You underplayed your role a lot and you weren't quite the innocent passenger you like to pretend. Although you did not repent after the first robbery, the court accepts your sincere regret and it notes that you were dragged along."

When he hugged his mother, they both wept.

Manuel was released from prison after ten months when the high court set aside his sentence and instead remanded him into corrective supervision. After that, he became actively involved in his church.

The head girl

The tale of the Warmbaths farm girl, as it emerged from the evidence in court and from Dr Vollie Spies's report, was a tragic one. He got to know Tanya better over ten months than her mother ever did.

She received her first emotional blow when farm workers' children molested her. She was four and kept silent because she did not know how to tell her parents.

At the age of eight, a domestic of the family took her into a storeroom, undressed and fondled her, and threatened her into silence. She kept quiet once more, fearing rejection for not being able to say no.

She immersed herself in her schoolwork. Her hard-working and prominent father, Mark, had farms near Warmbaths (now Bela-Bela) and Settlers. He was her mentor and she worked hard to gain his and her mother Joey's recognition. Only 100% was good enough for her schoolwork. If she got 99%, her parents wanted an explanation for the missing 1%.

On the day that she was elected head girl of her primary school, her father revealed shocking news. He was deeply depressed and about to sell all his farms. Her role model had been toppled from his pedestal and her world was collapsing. Her father threatened to commit suicide and even to commit family murder.

The young Tanya tried to keep her father alive. He moved into a bedroom next to hers. "I could sense death every time I walked past his bedroom," she said.

She sat with him for hours in his darkened room, even when he was in the bath, and felt something die inside her too.

The family went for therapy and in September 1994, the psychologist indi-

> **She sat with him for hours in his darkened room, even when he was in the bath, and felt something die inside her too.**

cated that he wanted to see Tanya, then fourteen, alone. He molested and raped her in his consulting room. She refused to leave her room for days and kept silent about the latest abuse too. In the meantime, her parents battled with their own problems: her father's depression, approaching bankruptcy and marriage problems.

Later she confessed hysterically about the rape to her swimming coach. He told the school principal, who informed her parents. However, her father did not believe her and she received no support.

She buried herself in her schoolwork, won numerous academic prizes and in Grade 8 met an older boy.

But the emotionally neglected Tanya's new friend further rejected her. He also ill-treated her sexually. "I could not say no to him. I did it [sex] to keep him happy. When he was happy, I was also happy."

At fourteen, she started using alcohol to dull the pain of the relationship. Her parents divorced when she was sixteen. Her mother moved to Pretoria and Tanya became a school boarder at the Pretoria High School for Girls. Over weekends, she mothered her younger brother Kevin while her parents tried to start new lives for themselves.

At high school, she was promising and exemplary, excelling in sports and in her studies. In 1998, she was elected head girl of the residence and aimed to get at least four matric distinctions.

To gain financial independence she started working as a waitress over weekends in her matric year. However, the tips were too small and the delicate and attractive girl found work in Sunnyside as an escort. There, still a schoolgirl, she earned up to R25 000 a month.

Tanya Oosthuizen

As an escort, she was in control of her life. She could decide for herself who would get her body. "In a sick sense I found love in that way. Men noticed me and rewarded me."

Then, in 1999, she fell in love with the cocky André (Baby) Venter. "He was charming and dynamic. He appeared happy, the opposite of what I was," she later testified. Baby twisted her around his little finger and forced her to keep a diary. She, in turn, found out about his alleged car theft activities.

In July of that year, her world collapsed once more when she and Baby were arrested for robbing a video shop. She was released, but after being rounded up again in April 2000 following the string of robberies with her four boyfriends, the police confiscated her diary. All over it was written "Baby, I will love you forever".

Baby had apparently ordered her to note down all her daily movements in the diary. She even had to record when she went shopping and what she bought. She also had to note down a list of do's and don'ts in the diary.

She also had to note down a list of do's and don'ts in the diary.

73

Some of the do's were: *Talk to Baby until he says goodbye. Listen to what Baby says. Trust Baby. Calm Baby down when he is tense. Ask Baby if I can do something for him.*

Some of the don'ts were: *Don't put down the phone when Baby is talking. Don't be stubborn with Baby. Don't ask too many questions. Don't talk to other men.*

When he accused her of sleeping around, she had to write out lines like a schoolchild, sometimes 200 lines at a time. In the afternoons, she had to be home at five on the dot, when he would phone from prison on a cellphone. Liquor helped her to deal with Baby's demands. She started drinking at ten in the morning and drank before every robbery.

"I would have done anything for him," she said in court. "I felt guilty because he was inside and I was outside."

On 30 May 2001, after the sensational court case, Tanya was sentenced to 45 years in prison on three charges of armed robbery. Because the sentences were to run concurrently, it meant an effective 15 years in prison for her.

She wept as she embraced her father, who had attended the entire trial and had often sobbed aloud. Her mother Joey was there too, as was her stepmother Yvonne. Many of her former school friends as well as other friends heard the sentencing and some of the girls ran weeping from the courtroom.

Magistrate Kallie Bosch said, "You were previously arrested with André Venter for armed robbery. The case against you was withdrawn because you were willing to testify against him. You had your chance.

"The robberies by your little gang were well planned. You wanted to commit crimes.

"In your matric year you became a prostitute. No child can work for four distinctions while working as a prostitute.

"It was an unnatural relationship (with Venter) in which you allowed a criminal to give you lines like a Grade 1 child. You were afraid of him."

Tanya was admitted to the juvenile section of the women's prison at City Deep in Johannesburg. When she turned 21, she was transferred to the women's prison at Mondeor.

In August 2001, the high court reduced her sentence on appeal to an effective 12 years. The judges found, among others, that Baby Venter was obsessed with power and had exercised an unnaturally powerful influence over Tanya. He had not only controlled her life but had encouraged and advised her to commit crimes.

On 14 July 2004, Baby Venter pleaded not guilty to four charges of car theft, besides the later charges of robbing a video shop, theft, attempted escape and attempted murder of a policeman.

Three older men were charged with him, each on two counts of car theft. The foursome had allegedly responded to advertisements in order to steal cars.

By March 2006, Baby had been an awaiting-trial prisoner for six years. During that time, he had had seven lawyers.

He demanded to see Tanya and asked that she be brought to him to talk about her then statement in which she described the video shop robbery.

Baby also demanded to talk to witnesses in his court cases for eight hours a day, five days a week, and to be held in a single cell.

Mr Andries Lessing of the Department of Correctional Services' legal division said Baby Venter had exploited legal visits in the past for social calls. The state prosecutor, Mr Vleis van Zyl, said Baby was not to make contact with Tanya before any decision had been taken about whether she was going to testify against him.

Rugby, booze and blood

It would obviously have been nice to strike a golf ball like Eldrick (Tiger) Woods. But Tiger was a phenomenon: people thought he was born to play golf. At the age of three, he carded 48 over nine holes at the Navy Golf Club course in Cypress, California. In 1996, at twenty, and in his first year as a pro, he won the first two US PGA series tournaments, saying he felt he could win every tournament he played in. People did not believe him, thought he was bragging, but the following year, on 15 June 1997, he topped the world rankings.

By November 1999, the name Tiger Woods was on the lips of every golfer in the world, in each clubhouse, on every tee. Every schoolboy with a golf club dreamt of being the next Tiger.

In the pretty Free State town of Reitz, Ronnie Hunt and his sons were crazy about golf. Ronnie was an avid amateur and a committee member of the local golf club. He played off a low handicap and enjoyed the game along with his friends and sons. His eldest son and namesake, Ronnie, was a fine player in his own right. Then came Riaan, and the youngest at thirteen, Elro, had already inherited his father's love of the game.

The elder Ronnie did not play for glory but simply because golf offered him an escape. The endless satisfaction of hitting that one sweet shot compensated a hundred times over for all the others: the hook shots, the slices, the struggle to get out of the sand trap, the approach shots that stopped short or overran the green, the cold putter.

Ronnie did not want to win the US Masters; just occasionally he wanted to hit that one great shot that would make even Tiger Woods sit up and take notice.

On the weekend of 13 November 1999, he and a few friends from Reitz went to brave the monster course of the Lost City at Sun City in the Pilanesberg. It went fairly well over the first nine. At the tee of the short thirteenth, known as the crocodile hole, Ronnie drew his nine iron from

> **Ronnie did not want to win the US Masters; just occasionally he wanted to hit that one great shot that would make even Tiger Woods sit up and take notice.**

the bag. The par three hole was 145 metres and he should easily reach the green in one. With a bit of luck he could even get a birdie.

Ronnie excelled himself: he struck the ball perfectly. It soared high, dropped close to the hole, and before his very eyes and those of his companions, rolled into the hole. It was the perfect fluke.

At the clubhouse, he had to buy everyone a round and Tiger Woods was completely forgotten: very few players, especially those from Reitz, hit the perfect shot on the Lost City course. Even the pros did not. It was a highlight in Ronnie Hunt's life.

Ronnie Hunt senior

However, back home things were seldom that exciting. About three years after that perfect shot, a dreadful and tragic fate befell the Hunt family. Ronnie (49), his wife Elize (47) and Ronnie Jnr (26) were found dead in their Reitz home on Monday morning, 16 September 2002. All three had gunshot wounds to the head.

Two sons survived: Riaan (22) and Elro (16).

'The wrong friends'

Earlier in 2002, the year of the Hunt family murders that shook Reitz to its foundations, townspeople were saying that the devil had been let loose in their midst. There was talk of vandalism in the cemetery and of damage to child graves. They wondered about the big wooden door of the old Dutch Reformed church that had been set alight.

Policemen were sent for from Bethlehem to investigate occult activities among the children of Reitz. Speculation in the community was rife about a group of high school children, no more than teenagers, who allegedly abused alcohol, experimented with dagga and held late-night parties in the Reitz cemetery.

But why would small-town children go as far as vandalising child graves or setting fire to a church door? Even if a few beers had intoxicated them, all had decent upbringings and proper educations. Such behaviour was not consistent with a closely-knit, conservative community in a Free State town.

Policemen were sent for from Bethlehem to investigate occult activities among the children of Reitz.

Ronnie and Elize Hunt were worried about their youngest son, Elro. He was in Grade 10 and a boarder in the Ficksburg high school hostel. When he came home on weekends, he was constantly with friends. There were parties and there was drinking. Other parents also worried about the teenagers, but children were wilful and did not listen. Elro was one of them.

Elize Hunt

Ronnie decided to seek help. On Thursday, 12 September 2002, he phoned Dr Leon van der Linde, who was both a friend and the family doctor. Ronnie asked him whether he could visit him for a chat about Elro, about whom he was concerned. He was worried that Elro was mixing with the wrong friends and that they were drinking hard liquor.

The doctor knew Elro. He was a quiet boy who was not usually a difficult child and he loved golf. He also knew Ronnie's soft spot for his youngest son and he really wanted to help his friend. He agreed to see Ronnie at his rooms on the Monday to talk about Elro. It was always wise to find the underlying cause of a problem as quickly as possible and to treat it, even if it were an emotional rather than a medical matter.

Every parent of a teenager knew these problems: the moods and whims, the stubbornness, the wall of wilfulness that was impossible to breach.

Ronnie told Elize about his appointment for the Monday. She was also worried. Elro did badly at school and on weekends he partied. They had to do something. The two older boys were fine. Ronnie Jnr and Riaan had found their feet and both worked in Pretoria. Their lastborn was the worry.

Ronnie Jnr was visiting from Pretoria and perhaps it would be a good idea if he could speak to his younger brother. Perhaps a brotherly chat was what Elro needed.

On Saturday morning, Ronnie Jnr tried to talk to Elro about his friends and about his drinking. But Elro was on his high horse, telling his eldest brother those things did not concern him. He pocketed his cellphone and said he was going to watch rugby with friends that afternoon.

While Elro and two friends were watching a Currie Cup match on TV, each downed two beers and then opened a bottle of brandy. Elro's cellphone rang, but when he saw the caller was his father, he ignored the call and continued drinking.

After the game, the bottle of brandy was empty. Elro, only sixteen, was drunk as he walked home. In his befuddled mind, aggression was mounting. He knew what awaited him: the looming confrontation with his father who was waiting for him at home. His father had already talked to him about the drinking and hard words had been spoken, pleas and threats uttered.

His father and brother had also watched the match and had wanted Elro to join them. His father had two passions: golf and the Western Province rugby team.

Ronnie asked Elro why he had not answered his cellphone. Elro, drunk and aggressive, argued with him. Ronnie was furious and disappointed at the condition of his youngest son, and at his backchatting. He could smell the liquor and he asked Elro whether he had been drinking. Elro said yes.

The father slapped his son.

Elro stormed off, blinded by rage and humiliation, beer and brandy. He could take it no longer. Couldn't they just leave him alone? There was always this quarrelling about drink and friends.

Later that Saturday night, he drove his father's bakkie back to his rugby pals and to a teenage party where the liquor again flowed freely. Elro partied, laughed, chatted and drank while trying to forget about the quarrel with his parents.

One of the teenagers, a seventeen-year-old boy, took a car and drove through the town before crashing into a tree. He was charged with reckless and negligent driving, using a vehicle without the owner's permission, driving without a licence and ignoring a stop sign. He was released into the custody of his parents.

On Sunday, Elro avoided his parental home and visited his friends. That afternoon, they decided to drive to Bethlehem in the bakkie of Elro's father. They went to see a movie and ate in a restaurant, where each of them had another beer.

On Monday morning, Emily Mofokeng walked down Eland Road as usual to start her domestic chores at the Hunt house. She rang the doorbell but the house was deathly quiet. She rang again and was surprised that no-one came to open the door. She walked around the house and found a sliding door slightly open. The occupants had probably not heard her. Then she saw smears of something that looked like blood on the sliding door. She peered inside and saw more blood in the room.

Emily ran off to find help.

The police found three bodies in the house. Ronnie Jnr lay on the floor in the TV room. His parents were in the passage, with Ronnie Snr's head at an angle across his wife Elize's legs.

Ronnie Hunt junior

Two shots had killed Ronnie Jnr: one oblique shot in the face and another in the head. His father had been shot in the face and his mother between the eyes.

The police confiscated four shells. The neighbours whom they questioned had heard nothing suspicious that weekend and had not noticed anything untoward at the Hunts'. Someone had heard a muffled report and someone else noises like something breaking. One of the neighbours had also heard a faint cry, but had thought it might have been a howling dog somewhere in the neighbourhood.

After the investigation of the murder scene, the bodies were removed for postmortem examinations. The four bullets that had killed the three family members and the shells were given ballistic tests. It turned out they had been fired from a 6.35 mm pistol.

The murder weapon was nowhere to be found.

Ronnie's cellphone and his bakkie were also missing, and so was Elro.

Forgiveness in the cell

The gruesome murder of such well-known and respected residents deeply shocked the community. Ronnie was a salesman at a vehicle business and his wife worked for the Free State agricultural cooperative (VKB) in the town. And then their son, visiting from Pretoria, had also been slain. On Monday morning, dismayed colleagues and neighbours of the Hunt couple stood outside the house where the murders had occurred. They wondered at the cause of the terrible tragedy.

Riaan Hunt received news in Pretoria about the death of his parents and brother. He had been due to accompany his brother on the visit. However, work pressure prevented him from joining his family for the weekend. He left for Reitz, wondering about his youngest brother Elro, sole survivor of the tragedy.

The police murder and robbery unit investigated the murders. Apart from the leads in the house, it was important to trace the bakkie – there was little doubt that the bakkie would provide answers to many questions. The police asked a local radio station to help inform their listeners about the search for the bakkie.

Two inspectors, Riaan Kriel and Drikus van Barneveld, took part in the extensive police search. On Monday afternoon, they spotted the bakkie on the road to Bethlehem. They relayed the information on the police radio, and inspectors Gert van der Merwe and Danie Bierman of the murder and robbery unit arrived in a second vehicle to assist.

The driver of the bakkie noticed that the police were following him and he tried to speed off. On the old Tweeling road, he realised that he was not going to get away and he stopped on the roadside. The policemen were armed. The driver threw a firearm through the bakkie's window and said he was unarmed.

The sixteen-year-old Elro Hunt, his hair in a crew cut, wept as he was arrested.

A district surgeon took blood samples from him to test for alcohol and drugs.

The latest shock raced through the stunned community like wildfire and again prompted questions about the activities of drunken teenagers in the cemetery. The Bethlehem police who were investigating suspected occultist activities in Reitz among a group of schoolchildren could, however, find no link with the Hunt murders.

The next day, Tuesday, the dazed and tearful boy appeared in court.

Some of his Ficksburg school friends, both boys and girls, could not hold back their tears either. The learners from his school had arrived at the Reitz courtroom that morning with their principal and a few teachers to wait for him.

When Elro emerged from the courtroom in handcuffs, the children and teachers were allowed to have a quick word with him. The school principal, Neil Humphreys, said, "We have come to encourage him. He is a quiet boy who never caused any problems at school."

He said that although Elro was not gifted academically, he was in the process of finding his feet in a technical trade. The following term he would also have played in the school's second golf team for the final round of the league.

Humphreys gave Elro a Gideon pocket Bible on behalf of the staff. After the brief conversation and with the Bible clutched in his handcuffed hands, he was led away to a place of detention, a centre for juvenile offenders in Kroonstad.

A friend, a sturdy boy with blond hair, cried to see Elro being taken away. Other children also cried openly.

One of Elro's girl friends remarked, "I am so sorry for him. We lived next door to them for eight years. I can't believe something like this could have happened. Something must have made him snap."

Another friend said, "We got along well with him. He was a regular guy. The children cry when they talk about him."

Reitz high school pupils who knew Elro well were also at the court.

In Ficksburg, pupils wrote messages of support on a large green poster and sent it with a teacher to Kroonstad, to the centre where Elro was detained.

People remembered that at an early age Elro used to run to his mother and huddle against her whenever anyone spoke too loudly at home. His parents divorced when he was five but later they remarried.

While speculation continued about the motive for the murders, preparations were under way for the big funeral that Friday at eleven from the Reitz Dutch Reformed church.

Three new graves were dug a short distance from the recent grave of At Bouwer, co-owner and manager of the Royal Hotel in Reitz. He had been shot dead in a robbery only the month before. The peaceful town had not seen such violence and so many tears for a long time.

> **As the only survivors of the family, they wept and held each other. Riaan told Elro that he forgave him and that he would stand by him during the difficult times ahead.**

Shortly before the funeral, a moving scene took place in the cell where Riaan visited his brother Elro. As the only survivors of the family, they wept and held each other. Riaan told Elro that he forgave him and that he would stand by him during the difficult times ahead.

Commenting on the act of forgiveness, Dominee Piet Fourie said, "This was one of the finest things after all the dreadful events."

More than 400 people from all over the country paid their last respects to the Hunts that Friday. Everybody wondered what had happened.

Dominee Fourie said in his funeral service that what had happened at Reitz was like a bad dream. However, it was still a reality that could not be wished away. "We can only approach God with our heartache, our longing and questions. We may never receive answers to everything but we will be safe with God. May He grant each of us the strength and grace to learn from yesterday, to leave the past behind and look to Him for the future.

"We pray for Riaan and Elro, the two surviving brothers, who face a difficult road ahead," he said.

Riaan was distraught at the graveside of his parents. He stood at his mother's grave for a long time before the three coffins were lowered into the ground. He wept as he placed flowers on every coffin. Then he draped a Western Province rugby jersey over his father's coffin, after first clutching it to his chest for a long time.

Elro did not attend the funeral.

Dr Pieter Henning of Bloemfontein, brother-in-law of the murdered Elize Hunt, said people were devastated and heartbroken by the tragedy that had shaken the family to its roots.

"A family has been wiped out and the lives of all those who have been left behind have been changed completely. Apart from the unbelievable heartache that the loved ones have to deal with, there are the questions as to why it happened. It makes no sense and causes everyone enormous sorrow, and it makes the grieving process that much worse."

About Elro, he said, "People and teachers who knew him said he was a lively yet quiet and withdrawn boy with good manners. That which has transpired sounds almost impossible to reconcile with such a fine youngster who was loved by so many people."

Elro appeared in court again on the Wednesday after the funeral. Riaan was there as his brother's guardian. He and a lawyer, Christie van Wyk, applied to the court to have Elro referred to the Oranje hospital in Bloemfontein for psychological assessment. Some of Elro's school friends were at the court again to support him.

Later the court was requested that a social worker, Jakkie Mulder of the Kerklike Maatskaplike Diens (the church's social service), compile a report on Elro's background, the circumstances of his parental home, his present state and his "humanity". The report would influence the sentence, in the event of a conviction.

Riaan was present at each of Elro's court appearances. He supported him and visited him where he was being detained in Kroonstad.

Dominee Fourie, who had buried the Hunts and their eldest son, was also at the court and prayed with Elro.

After Elro had been in the Oranje hospital for a month, Riaan said, "He is doing well under the circumstances. He is better off in Kroonstad than in Bloemfontein [in the hospital for the mentally challenged].

"I am also fine but it is often still very difficult."

Other relatives who visited Elro said he was very quiet and he did not really talk. He was also noticeably thinner.

Austin Powers

In May 2003, Elro was tried in the circuit court in Bethlehem on three charges of murder and on various other offences relating to the events that Saturday afternoon. The hearing was held behind closed doors because he was a minor.

The proceedings started with tears. When Riaan appeared in the dock, Maria Motaung walked up to the silent Elro. Before Emily Mofokeng, Maria had worked for the Hunts as a loyal domestic for a long time.

She stood next to Elro and with her hand on his shoulder twice spoke his name softly, "Elro . . . Elro . . ." She looked him in the eye and enquired, "How are you keeping?"

With their eyes on each other, Elro choked up. When Maria started crying, Elro could also not hold back his tears any longer. A policeman led the grieving Maria from the courtroom.

Elize Hunt's sister, Riekie Henning of Bloemfontein, was also in court to support both brothers.

Elro, now seventeen, admitted to Mr Justice A P van Coller and two assessors, Mr Ludwig Diener Snr and Mr Koos de Beer, to shooting and killing his parents and eldest brother on 14 September the previous year in their home. He was convicted on three murder charges and on the illegal possession of a firearm and ammunition.

It was his father's slap and the accusations about his drinking with the wrong friends that had made Elro storm out of the TV room that Saturday afternoon after the rugby match. He felt guilty, but at that moment his young heart was full of hatred and his head full of alcohol.

Elro knew where his mother hid her 6.35 Astra pistol and bullets. He loaded the weapon and with it in hand, he walked down the passage, back to the TV room. There he ran into his parents, who had just left the room to look for him and to talk things through.

He simply lifted the pistol and shot his father point-blank in the face.

His father fell down and before his mother could escape or stop him, he shot her too. The bullet hit her between the eyes. His parents were down, his father's head halfway across his mother's legs. Both were dead.

His brother Ronnie Jnr came running and Elro shot him in the face in the TV room. Ronnie fell down but was not dead. Seriously wounded, he tried to get up. Elro walked up to his brother, pressed the pistol against his head and pulled the trigger again. Ronnie died.

Elro was half stunned by everything that had happened so suddenly, so quickly.

Now no-one could slap him, no-one could whine about his friends and his drinking. Now he was free to do as he pleased.

He took the keys to his father's bakkie and returned to his friends. There he drank some more and partied deep into the night. He laughed and chatted, not telling anyone about what had happened at his home that afternoon after the rugby. No-one knew about the three bodies lying there, no-one suspected that the mild-mannered, quiet boy had just shot and killed his own parents and brother.

Later that Saturday evening he went home. Avoiding the bodies, he looked for money and his father's cellphone, and returned to the party. That night he drove around aimlessly in his father's bakkie. Eventually he headed in the direction of Fouriesburg. There he found someone to buy his father's cellphone and he used the money to put petrol in the bakkie.

By Sunday morning, he was back in Reitz. Someone even thought he had seen Elro in church. No visitors or unexpected guests came to the Hunts' home in 5 Eland Road, in an upmarket part of Reitz. No-one discovered the bodies. Later that morning he was back with his friends. They decided to drive to Bethlehem, where a comedy film was showing that they wanted to see.

Elro enjoyed the movie. *Austin Powers in Goldmember* was the type of film that teenage boys found particularly amusing. It was full of crude and heavy-handed humour: Mike Myers played the roles of both Sir Austin Danger Powers and of his twin brother Dougie Powers, better known as Doctor Evil. Austin Powers was a parody of James Bond.

After the movie, the boys went to a restaurant for a meal and had a beer each.

When the other boys drove back to Reitz, Elro headed towards Ficksburg, where he was a school boarder. On Sunday night, he slept in the bakkie at a filling station in Ficksburg.

Early on Monday morning, he drove to Bloemfontein. There his mother had family, an aunt of his, but he never got there. His head was in turmoil; his thoughts were with the bodies at home. He knew his life had changed irreversibly.

Elro still had his mother's Astra pistol and bullets with him in the bakkie. He considered suicide and in the afternoon he decided to drive from Bloemfontein back to Reitz to shoot himself at home.

In court he testified, "On the way I heard on the radio [in the bakkie] that the police were looking for the bakkie. I did not want them to find me, so I removed one number plate.

"On a dirt road [near Reitz] I noticed the police following me. I stopped and threw the firearm out of the door so that they would not shoot me. Then I was arrested."

Inspector Gert van der Merwe, the investigating officer from the Bethlehem murder and robbery unit, testified, "It seemed as if Elro had put the pistol to his head in the bakkie [before throwing it out]. He said at the scene that he was on his way home, where he was going to shoot himself."

Dr Janus Pretorius, a psychiatrist at the Oranje hospital in Bloemfontein, testified that Elro had a subaverage IQ but that he was accountable.

Dr Van der Linde, the family doctor and friend of the Hunts, testified that Ronnie and Elize had been divorced. After remarrying, they worked hard at their marriage. "They were a normal country family. Ronnie was a sincere and honest person. In twenty years I never saw him drunk."

He said he knew Elro as a gentle child. "I discussed the events with his school principal and we simply could not make sense of them."

Professor Dap Louw, head of psychology at Free State University, testified that Elro had an average practical IQ and was good with his hands. However, his verbal or academic IQ – the basis for insight and judgment – was low. His level of maturity was also lower than one would have expected from his seventeen years.

Elro himself was unable to explain exactly what had really happened: his low verbal IQ and the liquor he had drunk had definitely affected his perceptions and judgment at the time of the murders.

Prof. Louw testified that Elro had told him that he would have liked to "turn time back by about four years because then alcohol and friends had not yet played a role".

Mr Justice van Coller sentenced Elro to twenty years in prison for each murder and another 28 months for the illegal possession of his mother's firearm and ammunition. He would have been in prison for more than 60 years. However, the judge ordered the sentences to run concurrently, which meant an effective twenty years behind bars for Elro.

The judge said research into violent crime and solutions thereto as well as into the disturbing alcohol abuse by

The judge said research into violent crime and solutions thereto as well as into the disturbing alcohol abuse by children in the country was urgently needed.

children in the country was urgently needed. He said it was distressing that teenagers were increasingly involved in murder. The state and the community had to intervene. He agreed with Prof. Louw that research was needed into the hosting of parties where liquor was freely available to children.

"Severe sentences are not the solution. The underlying causes of the problems have to be addressed. The community and churches have to help make money available for such research.

"These were three dreadful crimes. He [Elro] will have to live with this knowledge. Whatever possessed him to do it will probably never be explained."

The judge said Elro was young and could not be sentenced as an adult. However, despite his youth, low intellectual abilities, perception of unfair treatment, the humiliation of the slap, the liquor he had consumed and his remorse, he needed to serve a long prison sentence in the interests of the community.

Prof. Louw, with master's and doctor's degrees in criminology and psychology, and a visiting professor to various US universities, said there was no explanation yet why so many young people committed murder. Alcohol abuse among young people and students was a great source of concern.

In reaction to the events, Prof. Esmé van Rensburg of the school for psychosocial behavioural sciences at North-West University in Potchefstroom later said it was disturbing how many children were growing up today without structure or discipline.

"Many parents and teachers admit that they have no control over children any more. Some are even scared of children.

"Unfortunately the lack of control and discipline often has to be laid at the door of parents' own poor child-rearing methods."

Children can distinguish between right and wrong from an early age but only if they have been taught the distinction. "Morality is not built-in and is not inherited. The dilemma is that adults do not always consistently demonstrate to children what is wrong and what is right. For example: some adults argue that the use of dagga is wrong while others plead for its decriminalisation."

Boredom, poor judgment, prejudice, hatred, the absence of a non-violent role model show to a child how to deal with stress, violence in a community, and easy access to alcohol and drugs could also lead to crime.

The opinion of Prof. Anna van der Hoven of the department of criminology at Unisa was that violent children mirrored a violent society.

"South Africa is more violent and our statistics on violent behaviour are high compared with that of other countries. There must be discipline. Parents must be more consistent in the way they punish their children.

"One should not punish a child in such a way that one deprives him of his human dignity. When children go off the rails or commit crime, it is the result of inconsistent or overly severe discipline. If the father says yes and the mother says no, the child is confused."

Prof. Van der Hoven said parents had often been abused as children and they tended to repeat the pattern with their own children. They never learnt how to deal suitably with a situation. "Children who commit murder have often experienced serious violence and they are also exposed to violence on TV."

Prof. Van Rensburg also said the harmful effect of TV and TV games had been extensively documented. "Research by Mash & Wolfe (2002) indicates that children in the US have already seen 8 000 murders on TV and more than 100 000 other forms of violence by the time they reach twelve years of age.

"It is unclear what the situation is in South Africa. South African children may be exposed to less TV violence, but the situation may equally be worse because a lot of violence in South Africa is real and not TV fiction.

"Violence in either fiction or in reality desensitises children. The dilemma then is that they accept violence as normal. Even adult South Africans have been so desensitised that they simply accept it as part of their life."

Prof. Van der Hoven said one could recognise signs of violence in a child at an early age: there were substantial differences between naughty and violent children.

"A violent child will, for instance, torture an animal or kill it without any remorse."

Prof. Van Rensburg said children who had been emotionally neglected, abused or molested could easily develop emotional or pathological symptoms, or both.

"This does not necessarily lead to murder. It may take any form. Unfortunately, the public links emotional neglect and maltreatment with lower socioeconomic classes. Mr and Mrs Rich who never have time for their children are equally guilty of emotional neglect."

Parents often disguise this phenomenon by showering their children with expensive purchases or providing them with pricey hobbies – like hiring the most expensive private golf coach, for instance.

Death by ... drowning

They found the child's body in the water one Sunday morning, entangled in the reeds fringing the dam. There were traces of foam around the mouth. At first glance, that was the most striking indication of a drowning.

It was a tragic accident. The children had been warned to stay away but this boy came from the city. He did not know the perils of a farm dam and no-one had seen him struggling in the water, no-one had heard his cries for help. He could hardly swim.

A pathologist performing an autopsy in a case of unnatural death usually has three important questions in mind when the cause of death was drowning: Was the death really due to drowning? If so, was it suicide, murder or an accident? And, how long has the body been submerged?

The first question is the most important. If the person was dead before immersion in the water, it was naturally not a case of drowning. The boy, however, had traces of foam around the mouth, an indication that he was alive when he ended up in the water.

When someone drowns, water enters the airways along with air, where it mixes with various viscous secretions. A drowning person's panic-stricken attempts to draw breath forms a whirlpool of air, water and secretions in the trachea. Similar to soap, the secretions act as a surfactant and that forms foam. This foam leads the observer to the assumption that the person drowned.

However, an experienced pathologist knows that drowning is not the only cause of foam around the mouth and in the trachea. Foam also appears in some cases of epilepsy, electrocution and poisoning, and even in natural disorders such as bronchial oedema.

There is still another test: wipe off the foam and press on the chest. If more foam appears around the mouth, it is almost certain that the pathologist is dealing with a drowning. The vortex effect during the drowning process causes all the respiratory canals to fill with foam.

If the body has been submerged for a long time, though, no foam will be present, not even in the case of a true drowning.

In the absence of foam, the pathologist can perform another test to determine whether the victim has drowned. In water, especially dam water, there are certain single-celled plants called diatoms. They belong to the order *Diatomaceae*. Diatoms consist of a frustule, two overlapping valves that interlock around the cytoplasm. Diatoms are very small and visible only under a microscope, where they appear as clear, silvery symmetrical bodies. The valves happen to be extremely resistant to decay.

The principle of the diatom test is simple: a drowning person gasps for air, even while underwater. Together with the water and air, millions of diatoms end up in his lungs. The force with which a drowning person gasps for air causes capillaries in the lungs to rupture and diatoms to enter the bloodstream. The heart pumps the diatoms to remote regions such as the liver, brain, spinal cord and kidneys. Those organs can then be examined microscopically for diatoms in order to determine drowning. If a person was dead before entering the water, the diatoms could end up in the lungs through the hydrostatic pressure of water but they would not be able to spread any further.

Another important indicator of death by drowning, a pathologist would know, would be the presence of the cadaverous spasm. That is the persistence of the deceased's last physical action. This is usually found if the dying person was extremely agitated during his last moments and would clutch at anything. In the case of death by drowning, he would make frantic efforts to save himself and grab at the proverbial last straw, a reed in the water or a stone on the bottom. That would indicate that he was alive when he landed in the water.

To answer the second question, whether the drowning was suicide, murder or an accident, is more difficult for the pathologist. The most obvious way is to examine the body for external injuries, such as whether the drowning person was knocked unconscious before landing in the water.

Many such external injuries may, however, also have been caused after death, for instance by aquatic animals or a current carrying the body along. A swimmer may also bump his head or face against a rock or other hard underwater object, lose consciousness and drown.

The third question, concerning the duration of the body's stay in the water, is relatively easy to determine visually: when the fingertips are wrinkled, the body has been in the water for about half a day; wrinkled palms indicate two days; wrinkled soles of the feet, three days. After a week or longer the skin can be peeled off the hands and feet like a glove.

Little Isaac Miggels first saw the light of day in 1995 on the Cape Flats, the same year in which a young teacher, Norman Simons, was sentenced for the murder of the 11-year-old Elroy van Rooyen. The year of Isaac's birth marked the end of the Station Strangler's reign of terror on the Flats. The parents' hearts still ached, but they could dry the tears for a while.

Isaac was a little ray of sunshine in the lives of his parents, Jakobus and Elsabé Miggels. His two grannies, on both sides, could not wait for their grandson's visits. It was so much better, and safer, on the Faure farm than in the city. And it was not all that far to drive from Blackheath and Mitchells Plain to the Helderberg.

The two grannies soon had a nickname for little Isaac: Kleinkind. Whenever Kleinkind visited Faure, Hessie Miggels on the father's side and Sara Jeneker on the mother's side were all set to spoil him. There were also many playmates in the small, tightknit farming community to keep Kleinkind occupied and from under the feet of the grown-ups.

There was plenty of room to run around in, even a fine dam for swimming or boating. What more could a Flats child ask for, on that peaceful farm? It was so pretty too, the beautiful Helderberg basin surrounded by the mountains of Stellenbosch and Jonkershoek, and farther out the Groot-Drakenstein, Franschhoek and, towards Sir Lowry's Pass, the Hottentots-Holland ranges.

Faure was a lovely spot. It was full of history and beauty – not a place for Kleinkind to die in, so young and so cruelly.

> **Isaac was a little ray of sunshine in the lives of his parents, Jakobus and Elsabé Miggels. His two grannies, on both sides, could not wait for their grandson's visits.**

Doli incapax

The Latin legal principle of *doli incapax* has been invoked since Victorian times, to protect naughty children against oversevere punishment when they unwittingly or simply in their childlike innocence break the law or some other regulation. Before the introduction of such legal protection, unruly street children were simply hanged.

Although *doli incapax* also applies in South African law, it gained renewed currency worldwide when it came under the spotlight in England only two years before the birth of little Isaac Miggels. It would later find application in his case.

A growing global trend – one also on the increase in South Africa – of young children committing violent crimes such as murder brought it to the fore. The legal principle assumes that any child younger than seven years is *doli incapax*: a child cannot be held legally responsible for an offence, even murder, because the child would have been incapable of grasping the consequences of its actions.

A child of between seven and fourteen years is also *doli incapax*, but based on a refutable assumption. Such a child cannot simply be pardoned but has to be subjected to a forensic evaluation of aspects such mental health, age and emotional and intellectual development, measured against indices of social competence.

In Liverpool, England, the principle of *doli incapax* was put to a highly publicised test.

Little Jamie was warmly dressed on the Friday afternoon of 12 February 1993. Over his Noddy T-shirt and grey tracksuit, he wore a blue windcheater with the hood pulled over his blond hair. Around his neck was a blue scarf with the design of a cat on it. February was the coldest month of the year in Liverpool on the Irish Sea.

Jamie had gone with his mother, Denise, to the Strand shopping centre in Bootle. He was niggly and restless, and wanted to go home. It was his birthday in three weeks, his third.

The shopping was done and all Denise still had to do was to buy cooked ham at the A R Tyms butchery. She rummaged in her bag for change and when she looked up again, her only child Jamie was gone.

Denise was hysterical and combed the entire shopping centre, but no-one remembered seeing a two-year-old in a blue windcheater. If he had been wandering around on his own, he would have been crying and someone would have noticed the lost child.

The police launched a massive search. Two days later, that Sunday afternoon, two boys looking for their lost soccer ball made a gruesome discovery on a railway line. They first thought it was a dead cat, and then it looked more like a doll. But when they saw it was a child, they ran to the nearby Walton Lane police station.

The police had found little Jamie Bulger.

It emerged from investigations and an autopsy that the two-year-old had 42 injuries to the body and face. He had, among others, been pelted with stones, kicked, beaten and molested. The unconscious child was then placed on the railway line to make it look like an accident. A train had hit him. The head and torso were still swaddled in the blue windcheater. The train had dragged his lower body several metres farther along the line.

Security cameras at the shopping centre provided images of Jamie leaving with two boys. The images were shown on TV news broadcasts worldwide.

The two boys were identified as Robert Thompson and Jon Venables, both only ten years old.

Which of the two was the instigator of such a dreadful murder? Could the two ten-year-olds distinguish between right and wrong?

It was argued in the boys' defence that neither had been involved in anything similar before. They had 'stolen' Jamie as a mischievous prank, with no thought of murder. After walking the streets with him for hours, during which time numerous people had seen them, they did not know what to do with Jamie. They did not want to abandon him. Then the game got ugly and they started hitting and kicking him, and worse.

At what age, lawyers asked, did *doli incapax* cease? At what age did children lose their innocence?

In the case of Jamie Bulger's murder, the court decided it was at the age of ten. They sentenced Robert Thompson and Jon Venables to be detained at "Her Majesty's pleasure" in a juvenile institution for an indeterminate period.

The two were released in 2001, with new identities and a lifelong court order prohibiting their new names from ever being made public.

Kleinkind

Isaac (Kleinkind) Miggels was an active little chap, and like children of that age, he did everything with enthusiasm and abandon. At eight, he had no worries. Besides, his parents were proud of him for passing Grade 2 as well as he did. Now the long summer holidays and Christmas lay ahead.

Excitedly he looked forward to his stay on the farm at Faure. He would make new friends and his two grannies would spoil him rotten.

Kleinkind arrived at Faure shortly after the schools had closed for the year-end holidays. He took turns sleeping at Granny Hessie's and Granny Sara's, their homes being within walking distance of each other. And a child could have lots of fun at the farm dam, although he had been warned to be wary of the water.

On Friday afternoon, 5 December 2003, Kleinkind was at the home of his Jeneker grandparents, Kupido and Sara. He helped Granny Sara collect kindling for the stove. He foraged busily and chatted all the time. He was especially excited

Isaac (Kleinkind) Miggels

about going to town with Granny Hessie the following day, the Saturday. She wanted to buy him new shoes. He told them about Granny Hessie's pretty tankards that one wound up so that they played tunes. He would amuse himself for hours with those wind-up mugs and listen to them spellbound.

He had also found three new chums more or less his own age. Two of them were possibly a bit older. They enjoyed playing together, especially around the dam.

Kleinkind had played himself to a standstill by the time he went to bed early that Friday evening.

Saturday morning he was up early, ready for a long day of playing. Granny Sara gave him his tea and a sandwich, which he gulped down before setting off soon after nine. He said he was going to Granny Hessie so that they could buy him those shoes.

Sara Jeneker was unconcerned about Kleinkind. He was safe with Hessie Miggels and was sure to pop up again some time or another at her and Kupido's, perhaps the next day or on Monday, or whenever. Let the child be, let him play, she thought.

However, Kleinkind did not arrive at Granny Hessie's that Saturday morning. She thought he must have been really enjoying his stay at Sara's house. The buying of the shoes could wait for another day.

On Sunday morning, Hessie strolled over to the Jenekers to inquire about everybody's welfare – and why was she seeing so little of Kleinkind?

The two grannies were immediately uneasy. It was not like Kleinkind to stay away just like that.

Sara was surprised when Hessie turned up to ask whether Kleinkind was still staying with them. No, said Sara, Kleinkind had left on Saturday morning already to go to Hessie's home. Was he not there?

The two grannies were immediately uneasy. It was unlike Kleinkind to stay away just like that.

Then a little chap came running up, wild-eyed. "Kleinkind is lying dead in the dam! Kleinkind is lying dead in the dam!" he shouted in a shrill, hysterical little voice.

Everybody set off for the dam in a panic. They found Kleinkind among the reeds along the shore. The grannies were hysterical and there was pandemonium in the small farming community.

Someone called the police and police divers retrieved Kleinkind's body from the water. They examined the environs at the dam: there were children's footprints everywhere. It seemed like an accident, as if

Kleinkind had gone into the dam and had drowned. And everyone had warned him!

Jakobus and Elsabé Miggels, parents of four children, were inconsolable. Their little Isaac had to leave the Flats for the security of the farm and had to die there.

The children who were questioned confirmed that they had seen Kleinkind and three playmates go down to the dam on Saturday afternoon.

The three playmates were identified and questioned. They were seven, nine and ten years old. Yes, they had played with Kleinkind at the dam on Saturday. Then he had left. They did not know what happened after that.

The playmates appeared deeply shocked: their eyes were wide, their hands were clenched, and they were uneasy. However, that was understandable with the drowning of a child.

An autopsy revealed the characteristic signs of drowning: foam around the mouth and diatoms in the organs. He was alive when he landed in the water.

His fingertips were wrinkled; he had been in the water longer than 12 hours. The marks on the skin of his neck and throat could have happened postmortem or he could have hurt himself in his desperate struggle to keep from drowning.

After the first autopsy, Kleinkind's death was ascribed to unnatural causes, probably due to drowning.

The deeply saddened family started arranging Kleinkind's funeral. They had to say farewell to the lively little boy who had been taken away from them so suddenly and so cruelly.

However, on Wednesday, three days after the discovery of the body in the dam, the Faure community received another shock. The ten-year-old friend who had been playing with Kleinkind and the two other boys at the dam on Saturday told Bettie Hendricks in passing about the quarrel between the four of them at the dam.

He said they had quarrelled and then there had been a scuffle. Kleinkind had insulted their mothers and so they had hit him.

Bettie was Granny Hessie Miggels's neighbour, and Bettie told her of the fight. Hessie, in turn, told her son Jakobus, Kleinkind's father.

Jakobus smelt a rat and went to the police. In view of the ten-year-old's reference to the fight, he insisted that another autopsy be performed on his son before the funeral.

The second autopsy, done more comprehensively in view of the possible violence, revealed ominous signs. After examination of Kleinkind's skull, it appeared that he had received a violent blow to the head. His skull was opened and signs of bleeding on the brain were found. His Adam's apple was crushed and his face bore traces of a vicious blow. The injuries had probably been delivered before he had landed in the water. He was probably unconscious when he drowned.

Instead of a drowning accident, the police found themselves suddenly investigating a far more serious crime, perhaps even murder.

The three playmates were questioned once again. Bettie Hendricks was also questioned about what the ten-year-old boy had told her.

The fight

Years after Kleinkind's death, it is still unclear precisely what transpired that Saturday afternoon at the dam. Only the four boys would know: Kleinkind, eight years old and dead, the boy of seven, the boy of nine and the boy of ten. Each of these three told a different story.

It was impossible for the police investigators to determine from the children's explanations a correct chronological sequence of actions and times. It was frustrating because in investigating a murder, especially that of a child, facts such as motives, leads, witnesses, murder weapons, and a murderer were important.

The forensic picture of the events at the Faure farm dam was unclear.

The motive could have been that an eight-year-old had insulted the mothers of the three friends. Was such a motive strong enough for murder? Had a slap or two, or worse, been doled out during the violent argument? Were the altercation and the scuffle so serious that the three boys were scared of the consequences if Kleinkind were to complain?

The leads were a stone, a length of plank and a boat, and the footprints of four barefoot boys that placed them all at the scene of the crime.

Did they only hit him or was there murder in their young hearts? Did they realise that they had injured him so badly that he could die? Did they want to make his death appear like an ordinary drowning, as the initial assumption was?

Who took the lead? There must have been a leader. In the trial of Jon Venables and Robert Thompson for the murder of Jamie Bulger, leadership became a pertinent matter in court. Neither Venables nor Thompson would have been capable of such a cruel murder by himself. One had to have taken the lead, egging on the other to join in committing the murder.

At Faure, one of the three suspects must have taken the lead after the initial slapping and hitting. Someone must have said: Let's throw him into the dam, let's drown Kleinkind. If we don't drown him, he will complain and we will get a hiding. Let's make it look as if he drowned in the dam by accident. Let's take him into the dam and make it look like an accident.

However, people such as Kleinkind's father and policemen thought that the three young boys were incapable of hatching a plot like that. That raised another question: Did the boys get help or advice from an adult?

One theory suggested that after their struggle, when Kleinkind was lying unconscious next to the dam, they had panicked and confessed to an adult whom they knew they could trust. He or she had then guided them in the conspiracy.

It appeared that Kleinkind had left Granny Sara that Saturday morning, after his customary cup of tea. He had been on his way to Granny Hessie's to buy shoes.

> **That raised another question: Did the boys get help or advice from an adult?**

Along the way, he met three playmates. They said they were going to the dam to play. It sounded enticing. Playing at the dam was much better fun than going to shop for shoes. He let himself be talked into going to the dam.

The four boys had a fine time playing at the dam. They nattered on about all the things that interest youngsters of seven, eight, nine and ten. Then someone made an improper remark and someone else responded. The three boys were established friends and inhabitants of the closeknit farming community. Kleinkind was the outsider from town. There were two camps and although Kleinkind was in the minority, he was not at a loss for words.

However, it went beyond words. The ten-year-old suddenly took offence, found a rock and bashed Kleinkind on the head. Then the herd instinct took over: the nine-year-old had a plank, which he swung at Kleinkind, hitting him across the face and against the throat. The seven-year-old was also part of the peer group and he felt he had to do his bit. He boxed Kleinkind on the nose.

Kleinkind did not stand a chance. He fell down unconscious. The blow with the stone had caused brain haemorrhage, the plank had crushed his Adam's apple, and the punch to the nose had spattered his blood.

Bettie Hendricks said the ten-year-old had confessed to her, "He said he had hit him (Kleinkind) on the head with a rock. The other boy (of nine) hit him across the face with a plank. The little one (of seven) boxed him on the nose so that it bled."

The three young assailants looked at the unconscious boy. They were taken aback by the sudden violence and by what had happened. They wondered if Kleinkind was dead; he lay so still.

Suddenly all their aggression was replaced by fear. What was going to happen? What had they done and what were they going to do?

No-one knew.

They left Kleinkind there and set off for a deserted industrial site, where they hid for a while. Everything was quiet on the Saturday afternoon. With pounding hearts, they sat around wondering about Kleinkind.

There are several different accounts of what happened next.

Was dusk on Saturday the point at which they left their shelter to seek adult advice?

Alternatively, did they sit in their hideout, discussing their plan to make Kleinkind's death seem accidental?

It appeared that the boys had gone back to the dam at dusk, with or without advice. They loaded Kleinkind's body into a dinghy and rowed out to the middle of the dam. They tilted the boat to make him roll out and they watched as he disappeared below the water.

Then they went home, extremely nervous.

Early on Sunday morning they were back at the scene of the crime. To their horror, they saw Kleinkind's body washed up on the shore for all to see. They then decided to hide him among the reeds, which was where he was discovered later that morning.

Instigator

The grief-stricken parents, Jakobus and Elsabé Miggels of Blackheath, wanted to know who had instigated the murder of their little boy.

"We don't have much money but we want answers. Our child's murderers don't belong in our community," Elsabé told a newspaper. She particularly wanted to know where the children in question "had got the idea to dump Isaac's body in the dam in the early hours of 7 December, after he had been almost mutilated that Saturday".

Elna de Beer, a provincial police spokesperson, would not say how many children had been involved in the murder or even whether an adult had played a part. It later turned out

Die Burger

Granny Hessie Miggels at the farm dam

that a fourth boy, a younger brother of one of the three suspects, had also been questioned as he could also have been at the scene.

In the meantime, the director of public prosecutions had to decide whether to prosecute the three children. The three played on happily in the community where the tragedy had occurred, oblivious of the legal issues raging around their heads.

The mother of one of the boys who had been at the dam with Klein-kind said she was shocked by the allegations against her child. Another mother said she was distressed because her son had always been very quiet. She could not imagine such young children doing something like that. "I wondered on Saturday afternoon what they were up to because my son came home once, asked for bread and then left again. He seemed very nervous."

The 62-year-old Mrs Hessie Miggels, a widow, said she bore no grudges against her grandson's attackers. "I am a praying grandmother," she said.

While the police continued their investigations and decisions were being made about the fate of the children, Granny Hessie regularly showed pictures of Kleinkind to the three boys suspected of his murder.

"I showed them the pictures and told them that Kleinkind was in Heaven."

It troubled her that the investigation was so drawn-out. She wanted closure

The 62-year-old Mrs Hessie Miggels, a widow, said she bore no grudges against her grandson's attackers. "I am a praying grandmother," she said.

so that they could continue with their lives. She thought Kleinkind had been "buried" in the dam because it was thought his body would not surface again. As a religious person, she had to forgive and not harbour hatred in her heart.

"The child must rest. We can't still be bothered with lawyers."

In the meantime, the police were on tenterhooks about how to deal with media questions concerning the sensational case. There was reference to the legal principle of refutable *doli incapax*. In terms thereof children aged between seven and fourteen were not accountable unless there was sufficient evidence for disproving the possibility of acquittal in a trial.

Another provincial spokesperson, Captain Rod Beer, said children were not accountable for crimes. Children older than fourteen were treated as adults, while younger ones were either sent to a reformatory or reprieved.

Capt. Eugène Sitzer, a police spokesperson for the Eastern Metropole, said although the charge had switched to murder after the receipt of new information, no-one had been charged. The boys were also questioned in the Somerset West police station, but there was no confession of murder.

The investigating officer, James Robertson, said he had a watertight case.

For the first time, there was reference to the murder of two-year-old Jamie Bulger in Liverpool. Jon Venables and Robert Thompson were tried as adults for his murder and they were detained for eight years. They were ten years old when they killed Jamie.

Then, in the middle of the legal drama, another similar event occurred, in April 2004, barely four months after Kleinkind's death.

The police questioned three primary school boys from Belhar after the body of their twelve-year-old friend was discovered in a dam near a cemetery. Police divers found the body of Ashwill (Olla) Joseph after one of his friends admitted to his mother that they had dumped him in the dam.

Ashwill was allegedly drugged and had presumably drowned.

He and a group of friends had gone to sniff glue that Sunday afternoon at the Belhar cemetery, the boys told the police. When Olla lost consciousness, the boys took fright, dumped him in the water and watched as his body slowly sank to the bottom. Amanda Joseph, Olla's mother, watched in horror as her child's body unexpectedly floated to the surface during a search of the dam.

After the second incident, Dr Johnny Wait, a lecturer in child psychology at Stellenbosch University, said there was an increase in deviant behaviour among the youth.

Factors such as alcoholism, poverty and the absence of strong role models usually played a key role in the behaviour patterns of young people. "The community has reason for concern," he said.

In the meantime, the murder charge against the three boys in the death of Kleinkind was withdrawn in the Somerset West magistrate's court. The stipulation was that they follow a programme prescribed by the public prosecutor. The boys' parents also had to attend a rehabilitation programme in Lynedoch at the Sustainability Institute.

Leila Falletisch, a social worker at the institute, said the programme included reconciliation with the Miggels family.

Some months later, events took another turn when a newspaper reported the imminent investigation into the role of a father of one of the accused in Kleinkind's death. However, no evidence of that could be found.

Adv. Annette de Lange, senior counsel at the Western Cape public prosecutor, said among the reasons for withdrawing the murder charge against the children was their youth and the contradictory versions of the events. "There was also doubt about their ability to grasp the court proceedings because of their mental developmental level."

Psychologist Anne-Marie Rencken-Wentzel said it was very difficult to determine what the children had been thinking that day. They could even have been playing a fantasy game, or one of the boys with a personality disorder could have played a leading role in the events.

Mr Deon Ruyters, an expert in child development at Nicro (National Institute for Crime Prevention and Reintegration of Offenders), thought the murder would not have been committed without a leader. "Such a leader was probably one who had been exposed to more violence than the other children, whether at home or in his community."

Whenever a child or a group of children committed a murder, people blamed the mass media and children's exposure to TV violence. Ms Rencken-Wentzel and Mr Ruyters agreed that the mass media could play a role. However, people who disagreed with that argument pointed out that children from poor rural families seldom had access to such technology.

But Mr Ruyters said research showed that even the poorest of the poor in South Africa had some access to TV. Incidents of violence could, however, not be ascribed solely to the influence of TV programmes. In many cases poverty led to frustration among adults and that expressed itself in violence and in crimes such as rape, murder and assault. Children exposed to such hostility, he said, would also turn to violence more easily.

The absence of a father figure was often the reason why children joined gangs. In a gangster environment, it was expected of the gangsters to commit crimes. In such cases, Ms Rencken-Wentzel said, leadership figures and peer groups exerted considerable pressure on children to commit crimes. They feared rejection by their friends.

"If a child does not acquire problem-solving skills, his 'reptilian brain' kicks in. He reacts to primitive instincts and will fight rather

"If a child does not acquire problem-solving skills, his 'reptilian brain' kicks in. He reacts to primitive instincts and will fight rather than flee."

than flee," said Ms Rencken-Wentzel. On his own, a child would turn his back on a situation where problems occurred, but in a group, he would participate in order to avoid status loss.

She referred to research by Piaget, Kohlberg and Rosen (www.mentalhelp.net/psyhelp) regarding the various phases of moral development in children. Children between one and five years of age acted in a manner aimed at keeping them out of trouble because they wanted to avoid punishment.

Children between five and ten did not respect the rights of others but would share, hoping to gain something in return.

Between eight and sixteen children did not want to do those things that pleased only themselves. They also wanted to please other people and conformed in order to meet others' expectations. That phase could overlap with the phase of children between five and ten.

By the age of sixteen, most children had accepted their community's code of conduct and felt themselves obliged to conform.

At ten, a child should start acting according to certain moral guidelines. Even a younger child would already know what was right and wrong, although he might at times not be able to keep himself from hurting a playmate. A child younger than ten did not understand the permanence of death.

Regarding the possibility of rehabilitating child murderers at such an early age, Ms Rencken-Wentzel said, "If a child is a sociopath, moral development does not occur as it should and it is incredibly difficult to rehabilitate him. It is vastly important for children to have positive role models with whom to identify."

Amy's magic

Elliot was hardly a man of means, but he considered himself a good father. He was strict with his children and tried to raise and guide them by wisdom and example. He never had opportunities such as those of his children, but no-one looked down on him. He was a conscientious and hard-working gardener at the Old Mutual and he hoped his children would recognise those qualities.

He gave them a roof over their heads, however modest, and food and clothing. All he hoped for was that they would treat their parents with consideration and not be lost to them. The young people were the so-called lost generation: so many of them had simply disappeared, swallowed by the dark tide of hatred and bloodlust sweeping the country.

Elliot was especially proud of his son Mzikhona. He was a good child and a diehard who wanted to complete his schooling and not work as a gardener. He was a bit older than his classmates in Joe Slovo High School on the Cape Flats. Mzikhona was no trouble as a child and his nickname Easy suited him well. Elliot believed his son Easy was going to go places.

Of course, the father knew about the political agitators who were planting the seeds of resentment and aggression among pupils and students. In 1993, those receptive young minds were fertile soil. The father knew all that and it brought anxiety to his mind.

He was fully aware of all the injustices that had been perpetrated and were still being perpetrated, of the bitterness about apartheid, the suffering, humiliation and denigration. It was a hard burden for anyone to bear. He had endured it but he could understand the anger of the new generation who wanted to claim their just and equal share in the country of their birth. It was their right.

The release of Nelson Mandela and talk of democratic elections the following year brought hope, Elliot thought. Then he, too, Elliot Nofemela, gardener and father, would draw his cross on a ballot for the first time – as a full citizen of his country.

Never mind the humble little house he called home, held together by hope and wire, or that he lived in Guguletu on the Flats. The name of his street was NY111 for "Native Yard" – a tag that rubbed salt into the wounds of one's rejection.

Never mind that there was little hope afoot in Guguletu and also in Langa, Khayelitsha, Nyanga, Browns Farm and all the other seething and simmering ghettos.

Easy was at school and had good friends, his father thought. His girl-friend, Nompinki Mayekiso, often visited their home. Further down the same road lived Easy's bosom buddy, Ntobeko. Easy and Ntobeko had grown up together in NY111 and Elliot knew Ntobeko's mother, Georgina Peni, a good woman with great hopes for her children too.

The two friends did not attend the same school. Ntobeko was in Langa High, where the Paso meeting was that day, the meeting Easy had mentioned.

The meeting

It was important for Easy to be involved in the Pan Africanist Students' Organisation (Paso). Unlike his father, he was not going to sit around and wait for something to happen. He believed his salvation and the solution lay with the Pan Africanist Congress (PAC). The Azanian People's Liberation Army (Apla) cadres of the PAC had demonstrated their willingness to continue with the struggle, to let blood flow for liberation. They were not going to sit around the table like the African National Congress (ANC) and bandy about many fine words concerning the future.

However, Elliot was ignorant of Easy's true involvement in township politics and in the PAC. He did not know that Apla operatives were training Easy and Ntobeko. They attended political lectures, and in the afternoons, there were physical training and demonstrations in the use of firearms and ammunition.

The leaders had noticed Easy and he was proud of being appointed a Paso organiser. He and the other organisers had invited pupils from all the neighbouring schools to that day's meeting at Langa High. The turn-out was good.

By one o'clock that Wednesday, 25 August 1993, almost 400 pupils had gathered at the school to form a new branch of Paso. Easy was pleased when Ntobeko, eighteen years old and in Standard 8 (Grade 10), was elected chairman.

One Mongesi Manqina (20) and in Standard 6 (Grade 8), was elected vice-chairman.

Easy and Ntobeko did not yet know Mongesi.

The path of another boy in the throng of children would cross theirs a few hours later. They did not know Vusumzi Samuel Ntamo either. He had managed to pass only Standard 4 (Grade 6). School was no big deal for him.

Soon it was the turn of the main speakers, for whom everyone had been waiting: Simpiwe Mxengu, regional secretary of Paso, and Wanda Mathebula, regional chairman.

The speakers were militant and inflammatory, and the children cheered them. They toyi-toyied, sang liberation songs and felt their blood rising. In addition, the speakers were saying what the children wanted to hear: it was not only Apla's war to regain the country for black people. Each one of those present, the youth, had to participate.

All the Paso members were ordered to help the Apla operatives at ground level make the country ungovernable.

They heard that 1993 was the "Year of the Great Storm". The children at the meeting were told that all Paso members had to fulfil that Apla slogan. They embraced it enthusiastically.

Paso members were also expected to recognise the teachers' strike and to refuse to pay examination fees. The purpose was to destroy the whole education system, the speakers said. That would help force the white rulers to hand the country to the black people, to whom it belonged. The project was known as Operation Barcelona and was promoted under the auspices of the Congress of South African Students (Cosas), which was affiliated to the ANC. The pupils accepted those proposals to great acclaim too.

All the speeches were concluded with numerous and challenging exclamations of the inflammatory slogan "One settler, one bullet!"

All the speeches were concluded with numerous and challenging exclamations of the inflammatory slogan "One settler, one bullet!"

The children at the meeting understood that the slogan applied to every white person crossing the line of fire of an Apla operation.

In the combative atmosphere rampant that Wednesday afternoon, they also understood that the slogan "One settler, one bullet!" meant that any white person crossing the path of Paso members supporting the Apla operatives in making the country ungovernable would be fair game.

The meeting dispersed at about three that afternoon, amidst singing, shouts of "One settler, one bullet!", and toyi-toying.

Easy and Ntobeko were in a group of about 200 children making their way to the Bonteheuwel railway station. The remainder, mostly Langa residents, stayed behind and wandered through the neighbourhood streets.

Easy's group walked singing and dancing down Vanguard Drive towards the station. They picked up stones and hurled them at cars. They stopped a truck and the terrified driver fled from the enraged youths. They pelted the truck with stones, tried to overturn it and set it alight.

When a police van arrived, the youths shattered its windscreen with stones. Shots were fired and the mob scattered. About 80 youths who had congregated in a smaller group arrived at the Bonteheuwel station.

Easy and Ntobeko were part of the group who boarded the train. They rode past the Natrec station and got off at the Heideveld station.

It was already after four that afternoon and it was not far from Heideveld to the homes of Easy and Ntobeko in NY111.

Their group was still buzzing after the day's events. They kept singing and shouting the inflammatory slogan. They toyi-toyied past NY110 towards NY1, which was the main road through Guguletu. They carried stones and half bricks, and they were on the lookout for targets: state and private vehicles. When they found nothing, Easy and Ntobeko peeled off to the Iona shopping centre in NY1.

At the centre, Ntobeko spotted a red bakkie. He knew the driver, one Maleleke, who worked at the Viveza shop in NY119. Easy and Ntobeko jumped onto the back of the truck. Maleleke and his co-driver were on their way to the shop where he worked, in Guguletu's section three and not far from the parental homes of Easy and Ntobeko.

They drove along NY1. On the corner of NY1 and Klipfontein Road, just beyond the BP filling station, Easy and Ntobeko saw a group of youths crowding together and singing.

Further along, near the Caltex filling station on the corner of NY1 and NY132, they saw another group of children throwing stones at a truck and at a Mazda car behind the truck.

Then they saw a young white woman jump out of the Mazda and run across the road. She cried as the stones hit her. Her face and head were already bloodied.

The crowd of youths lusted after blood and shouted after the bleeding, stumbling woman, "One settler, one bullet!"

Easy and Ntobeko jumped off the bakkie.

Her last journey

Amy Biehl, in contrast to Easy, Ntobeko, Mongesi and Vusumzi, came from a privileged home. She was raised a Catholic in Costa Mesa near Newport Beach in California. She was one of three sisters and a brother.

At 26, she was the middle daughter. The others were Kim (27) and Molly (23). Zach (16) was the youngest.

Amy was an academic star in high school, and at graduation, she delivered the school valedictory speech on behalf of her class. At Stanford University, she gained her degree cum laude. The actress Reese Witherspoon, who later achieved fame for her roles in films such as *Legally Blonde* and *Walk the Line*, was also a Stanford graduate.

Amy Biehl

During Amy's political studies at Stanford, some of her professors stimulated her curiosity concerning Africa. She was especially interested in Namibia and South Africa, and in 1989 she was an observer in Windhoek in the Namibian elections.

Amy, attractive and bright, had strong personal principles. She believed intensely in a free democracy and especially in the role of women in such an open society. When she was awarded a sought-after Fulbright scholarship from Stanford to visit South Africa, she jumped at the opportunity. She convinced her boyfriend, Scott Meinert, who had been thinking about marriage, to wait a while. She and Scott had met at Stanford as students.

Everybody who knew Amy predicted great things for her. Her parents, Peter and Linda, were convinced that she was destined for an academic career as a university lecturer.

At the end of 1992, she arrived in Cape Town on an exchange programme at the law centre of the University of the Western Cape (UWC). On her first visit to South Africa, she wanted to assist in setting up a black voter registration programme for the country's first democratic elections in April 1994. She also wanted to devote herself to women's rights, especially among the disadvantaged women of the country.

She and her mother Linda did not write to each other very often but preferred to chat on the phone. Her parents had never been to South Africa. However, they were aware of political events in the country and the great expectations of a new political dispensation after the long and bitter years of apartheid.

In letters to her best friend, Miruni Soosaipillai, a lawyer in California, Amy wrote about her stay in Cape Town. She also wrote about finishing the Comrades Marathon in 10 hours and 24 minutes. "I am learning Xhosa and you should hear me making those clicks," she wrote.

She also spoke in her letters about Packo, a Mozambican drummer with whom she sometimes went jogging. "You should see the dirty looks we get from whites. Apartheid isn't dead yet!"

In July 1993, she wrote to Miruni about her attempts to obtain study funds for a South African friend, Maletsatsi. "We tried to get [her] a bursary from an elite women's club. But those white women do not understand that her [Maletsatsi's] poor tuition is the result of their racist education policies."

At about that time, Amy received good news – she heard that she had been awarded a Jacob Javitz study grant for doctoral studies at Rutgers University in New Jersey. It was with mixed feelings that she started packing at the end of August and booked her flight back to California for Saturday, 28 August 1993. She wanted to spend just one day at home with her parents after her long absence in South Africa before starting at Rutgers that Monday.

But then, only three days before flying back to a bright future, Amy made a fatal decision.

But then, only three days before flying back to a bright future, Amy made a fatal decision. Late that Wednesday she offered two student colleagues at UWC a lift to their homes in Guguletu.

The two women, Sindiswa Bevu and Maletsatsi Maceba, got into the back of Amy's mustard-coloured Mazda 323. Maletsatsi was the student for whom Amy had battled so hard to find study funds.

The nineteen-year-old Everon Orange sat next to Amy in the front. He did not live in Guguletu but went along for the ride. He had known Amy since her arrival in the country ten months before.

Their excited chatter in the car was tinged with sadness about Amy's return to the US on Saturday. Only three days were left before her departure. However, Amy had not seen her parents, sisters and young Zach for months, and Scott was also waiting.

She was wearing blue jeans and a white top. Her blonde hair flowed over her shoulders and a smile always wreathed her lips.

At about five o'clock, her Mazda turned into NY1. She was unaware of the Paso meeting earlier that afternoon at Langa High. She was unaware of the inflammatory speeches. She did know of the tense situation in the townships, of the seething hatred and resentment, of the boil about to burst wide open. Still, she felt at ease. She was regarded as a comrade, as someone who cared for the people who had suffered over so many years.

However, that day she did not know that she was carrying the stigma of a settler. She was unaware of the large groups of hyped-up children in the streets, singing and shouting "One settler, one bullet!" and toyi-toying. She was also unaware that they were throwing stones at cars carrying whites because every white was a target in the "Year of the Great Storm", aimed at making the country ungovernable and reclaiming it.

Amy did not think of herself as a settler. She was from the US and was in South Africa to help the comrades. She had not taken any land from black people and there was no reason at all to harm her.

As they approached the Caltex filling station in NY1, the atmosphere turned ominous and the four young people in the Mazda were suddenly worried. They noticed the toyi-toying youths in their Paso T-shirts and saw the truck in front of them being stoned and surrounded.

Suddenly a cry echoed down the street above the chaos, "Here comes a settler!"

The attention shifted from the truck to Amy with her white face and fair hair behind the Mazda's wheel. She braked to a halt when the first rocks hit the car. Then it was like a fierce hailstorm. The windscreen shattered, a stone hit her on the head. Panic-stricken, she was hardly aware of the blood.

Suddenly a cry echoed down the street above the chaos, "Here comes a settler!"

Next to her Everon hunched up against the stones. Maletsatsi and Sindiswa lay down in the back of the car to get away from the stones. Everon saw the terror in Amy's wide eyes.

A hand appeared at her window and ripped her watch from her arm. Everon pulled Amy's head down onto his lap to protect her against the assailants.

Then he saw her push open the door and run around the front of the car and across the road to the safety of the filling station. Behind her Maletsatsi and Sindiswa also jumped out and with hands held high, pleaded for Amy's safety because she was not a settler.

No-one listened and they pursued Amy like sharks in a feeding frenzy.

Everon feared for his life, but all the attention was fixed on Amy. He spotted someone at his side of the car. He asked what he had to do, what they were going to do to her.

The answer came: escape, they are not interested in you; all they want is the settler. Everon fled from the car to the filling station. He was a coloured man but was treated like a traitor. Maletsatsi and Sindiswa too had to duck from rocks and one was stabbed in the hand with a knife while being accused of being an *impimpi* (traitor).

Mongesi Manqina tripped Amy and she fell down in the street. A group of seven to ten youths descended on the defenceless and injured girl. They threw rocks and bricks at her, stabbed her with a knife, repeatedly kicked her and grabbed her by the hair while hammering her with a rock.

On the ground, she got hold of someone's arm. She wept and pleaded, "Please help me . . ."

No-one helped.

She got up, stumbled over a white wooden fence and collapsed next to a potted plant at the filling station.

Suddenly the police were there and the attackers took to their heels. Paramedics were summoned. One of them, Victor West, tried in vain to save the life of the bleeding girl.

She was helped into the back of a vehicle but died there of blood loss and the savage wounds to her head and body.

Schoolgirls at the scene cried hysterically about the spilling of blood they had just witnessed.

'Senzenina?'

In Newport Beach, Amy's parents received the telephone call informing them of their daughter's gruesome death. They could not understand it. Why Amy, who had loved South Africa so much and who had cared so deeply about the people in the townships?

Shortly after hearing the shocking news, her mother Linda said, "Everyone said such beautiful things about Amy. It makes one proud of one's child and takes away the worst heartache."

The family soon thought of erecting a living memorial to their daughter and planned to visit South Africa to see where she had worked and died. President Bill Clinton also phoned the Biehls to convey his sympathy.

On the Thursday, a day after her death, hundreds of friends attended a memorial service at UWC and sang a liberation song, *Senzenina? (What have we done?)*. Later that day a crowd walked the "last mile" along which Amy had driven to her death in NY1, Guguletu.

One of the posters read, "Comrades come in all colours."

"Comrades come in all colours."

110

People placed flowers and wreaths on the blood in the road and on the low wooden fence where Amy had expired.

That same day the investigating officer, detective sergeant Ilmar Pikker, arrested Easy at his parents' home.

On the Sunday, there was a memorial service in St Gabriel's Catholic church in Guguletu. The next day Amy's remains were cremated at the Maitland crematorium before being conveyed to the US.

On 8 October, seven young suspects, among them a boy of 15, appeared in the Mitchells Plain magistrates court regarding Amy's death. Among them were Mongesi Manqina, Vusumzi Ntamo and Easy Mzikhona Nofemela. Easy's friend, Ntobeko Peni, was not one of them.

During the court proceedings, PAC supporters threatened people and shouted slogans such as, "Long live the murderers of Amy Biehl! Long live!"

In November, the murder trial of Easy, Mongesi and Vusumzi started. The other suspects had been released.

Amy's white blouse, blue jeans and underwear were submitted as evidence in court.

A pathologist said that of the many injuries to her body, any one of three more serious wounds could have caused her death.

However, the probable cause of death was a stab wound to the left side, between the ribs and left lung right into the heart. A deep wound above the right eye had penetrated the eyebrow ridge and the eye socket. "One could see into the skull." The third potentially mortal wound was on the left side of the head. It was triangular and had probably been caused by a brick. At that wound, there were bone fragments on the brain.

The two head injuries would have caused her death due to bleeding on the brain, even if there had been no deep stab wound into her heart.

There were also numerous other wounds, contusions and abrasions on her body.

Maletsatsi testified that she and Amy had been good friends. Both had belonged to the national coalition of women. She was emotional as she described Amy's condition after the attack.

"Amy was sitting next to a pot plant at the filling station. Blood poured from her face. Everon and I picked her up and carried her to the police vehicle. She groaned." When Maletsatsi testified about Amy's groans, PAC supporters laughed aloud in court.

When the trial resumed in the Cape High Court in January 1994, Linda and her youngest daughter Molly were in court for the first time. A man shouting "Settler! Settler!" greeted them.

In his testimony, Easy said he had never been at the murder scene. He claimed that he had been home the whole day and his parents would confirm his alibi.

His father Elliot testified that PAC people suddenly started turning up at his house after his son's arrest. It was the first time that anyone from the PAC had been to his home. Elliott said his son's involvement in the case shocked him. He had not raised his children in that way. He said they did not discuss the case at home because his wife burst into tears at every mention of Easy's name.

Elliot attended his son's trial every day. He also visited Easy in prison and whenever he asked him how he felt, Easy cried.

In a later statement to the court, Easy said that Mongesi Manqina, chosen that day as new vice-chairman of the Langa branch of Paso, was the one who had stabbed Amy. "He squatted over her and stabbed her with a knife. He was proud because he had killed a white person."

Mongesi also denied being present at the murder scene. He said he and a friend, Ndlancomo, had been chatting at a tripe stall near the Heideveld station at the time of the murder. He even denied having been at school at all that day or at the meeting where he had been elected vice-chairman. He said he had been at home, building a hut on his mother's instructions.

> **Elliot attended his son's trial every day. He also visited Easy in prison and whenever he asked him how he felt, Easy cried.**

A woman identified only as Witness A to protect her against possible victimisation testified in September 1994 about Ntobeko Peni's involvement. "He repeatedly jumped on Amy and bashed her head with a rock."

Witness A also said that both Easy and Mongesi had stabbed at Amy with a knife.

Vusumzi Ntamo confessed in a statement that he had thrown bricks at Amy's head while she was lying on the ground.

Scot-free again

In October 1994, Easy Nofemela, Mongesi Manqina and Vusumzi Ntamo were convicted of Amy's murder. Their legal counsel, Advocate Justice Poswa, argued in mitigation that the PAC and ANC leaders who together had chanted slogans such as "One settler, one bullet!" should be held accountable for the three young murderers' actions.

He said, "The people who incited the three accused to commit the crime hold high positions today and freely walk the streets."

Judge President G Friedman said in his judgment that it was impossible to determine who had delivered the fatal stab wound. He sentenced all three to eighteen years' imprisonment and said the murder had been racially motivated. "The only reason Miss Biehl was killed was because she had a white skin."

On 13 January 1995, Ntobeko Peni was arrested at his parents' home in NY111, Guguletu, at four in the morning. In his trial, it was testified that he had held Amy by the hair while hitting her on the head with a half brick. He had also kicked her.

Mr Justice A J Lategan found Ntobeko guilty on 6 June 1995, and sentenced him too to eighteen years for the murder of Amy. The judge said, "It is beyond any sane person's comprehension that a member of the human species could sink so low as to murder an innocent and defenceless person in such a horrific manner."

Two years later, in July 1997, Amy's four young murderers appeared before the amnesty committee of the Truth and Reconciliation Commission. The hearing generated great international interest, especially in the US. Amy's parents also attended.

The four testified that the PAC slogan "One settler, one bullet!" and the encouragement "to regain the black man's land" had incited them on the day of the murder.

However, Robin Brink, who led the evidence, said, "You were like sharks that had smelt blood."

Mongesi Manqina testified first and admitted his part in the murder for the first time. "Amy Biehl stumbled out of the car and ran to the Caltex filling station. We chased after her. I tripped her, sat down in front of her and stabbed her with the knife in the left side. I assume the knife thrust killed her. I stabbed her because I saw her as a target, as a settler.

"I was inspired by the slogan 'One settler, one bullet!' I wanted to become an Apla operative and I regarded the instruction to make the township ungovernable as an order to kill white people.

"I am sorry for what I did, also for lying during my trial. I ask the Biehl family for forgiveness."

> **"I am sorry for what I did, also for lying during my trial. I ask the Biehl family for forgiveness."**

During cross-examination, Robin Brink asked, "Who specifically gave the order to murder white people?"

Manqina: "It was Simpiwe [Mxengu, regional secretary of Paso]."

Brink: "You had no pity in your heart that day?"

Manqina: "No."

Brink: "The reason you killed her was so that the government would abolish matric fees?"

Manqina: "Yes, that is correct."

Brink: "How could you imagine that by killing a single, unarmed young white woman you would achieve your aim with the examination fees?"

Manqina: "The government would react if a white person was killed."

Brink: "You wanted to send a message to that government that if they did not abolish matric fees the people would continue to murder unarmed, defenceless women who happened to stray into the township?"

Manqina: "Yes."

Mr Justice Bernard Ngoepe: "How could you think that the murder of a single person on that particular afternoon in Guguletu would change the whole South Africa and would cause it to be given back to black people?"

Manqina: "With the death of Amy Biehl we wanted the government to answer our grievances . . . if not, we would continue to make the country ungovernable."

Ngoepe: "You would have carried on killing more white people?"

Manqina: "If necessary, we would have done it."

Ngoepe: "In what standard were you [at the time of the murder]?"

Manqina: "I was in standard six."

Ntobeko Peni also confessed about his part in Amy's death: "I and [Easy] Nofemela were on a bakkie. We saw Amy Biehl running across the road. She was bleeding from the head. A group of seven to ten people pursued her. I jumped off the bakkie and threw stones at her when I was about three or four metres away. Nofemela also jumped off and threw stones at her.

"I took part in the murder of Amy Biehl and I ask her parents, family and friends for forgiveness."

During cross-examination he said, "One settler, one bullet!" was aimed at white people, regardless of gender. "We had no pity on white people. In our eyes a white was a white."

"We had no pity on white people. In our eyes a white was a white."

Brink: "If Mr Joe Slovo had been in the township that afternoon, would you have stabbed, stoned and killed him too?"

Peni: "No, I would not."

Brink: "Why not?"

Peni: "Everyone knew him."

Easy Nofemela also admitted before the amnesty committee that he had actively helped to kill Amy. He, too, asked Amy's family for forgiveness. He said the militant speeches at the meeting earlier that afternoon had incited them.

Mr Justice Andrew Wilson: "Yes, but that had happened at about one or two o'clock?"

Nofemela: "Yes."

Wilson: "You left the meeting, walked to the station, caught a train and it [the murder] happened at five?"

Nofemela: "Yes, that is true."

Wilson: "Why had you been so emotional all afternoon?"

Nofemela: "While we were throwing stones at a truck in Vanguard Drive, the police fired on us, white policemen."

> "It is for the South African community to forgive its own [people] on the basis of ubuntu and other principles of humanity."

Wilson: "Why were you emotional [later]? You were sitting on a bakkie on your way home. You saw this unfortunate girl running across the street, you jumped off, chased her, threw stones at her, and stabbed at her. Why?"

Nofemela: "Nothing could cool us down . . ."

At the end of the hearing, Peter Biehl addressed the amnesty committee. He said, "We [he and his wife] cannot oppose amnesty . . . It is for the South African community to forgive its own [people] on the basis of ubuntu and other principles of humanity."

On 28 July 1998, the amnesty committee pardoned the four murderers. A few days later, they were out of jail and back at home.

Easy and Ntobeko started working for the Amy Biehl Foundation shortly afterwards. One of its aims was to combat juvenile crime in Cape Town's disadvantaged communities that had suffered socioeconomic deprivation. It aimed to achieve that by approaching community development holistically.

One of the projects was to deliver cheap bread in Guguletu. Known as Amy's Bread, it cost 25 cents a loaf and Easy was one of the deliverymen. He rose at five in the morning, dressed in a bulletproof vest and distributed the bread. However, the bread project was abandoned in August 2001 in Guguletu as it was becoming too dangerous for the delivery people. In the Southern Cape, Jakobus Louw of the Amy Biehl bakery in Thembalethu, near George, was shot dead.

Shortly afterwards, in September, a cookie project was started. The first one kg package, known as Amy's Biscuits, was symbolically auctioned and Ntobeko bought it for R8. He was then sales manager for Amy's Bread.

Peter Biehl died of cancer in April 2002. A month later, Easy appeared with Linda at an international conference in Cape Town on the involvement of NGOs in community projects. When the day of Amy's death and Easy's subsequent confession and contrition about the events were relived, they had the guests from 41 countries in tears.

The Biehl family also gave South African film maker Anant Singh permission to produce a film about Amy's life and the actress Reese Witherspoon committed herself to the role of Amy Biehl.

Amy's brother Zach became project manager of the Amy Biehl Foundation. By 2003, some 120 people from the Cape Flats were working fulltime on the foundation's projects to promote conciliation, quality of life and communication. At ground level, the projects were called Amy's Magic.

Victor West, one of the paramedics at the scene of Amy's murder, was programme director of a first-aid project in the foundation.

In 2003, Easy and Ntobeko attended a congress in Missouri in the US with Linda.

The foundation lost contact with Vusumzi Ntamo.

Mongesi Manqina, the fourth condemned murderer and the one who caused Amy's death with the knife thrust, was convicted in October 2003 of the rape of a mentally disabled girl. The victim had the mental capacity of a five-year-old. The rape had taken place about a year after Manqina's amnesty.

Easy Nofemela and Linda Biehl

The police hunted him for a long time after he had changed his name to Mluleki Ngozi.

By 26 April 2007, on what would have been Amy's fortieth birthday, the Amy Biehl Foundation expanded its aid programmes in South Africa's poor communities. More than 8 000 youths benefited from it every day. Her family and friends were convinced that the foundation had contributed to a decline in juvenile crime in the country. The programmes embraced after-school care, sports development, literacy, music, first aid, Aids awareness, environmental conservation, and golf lessons. A school was named in her honour.

In the US, the foundation was involved in welfare and development so that Amy's dreams and memory would survive on both sides of the Atlantic.

Adam and Eve

Alta was a pretty teenager with dark blonde hair and blue eyes. Like so many other teenage girls, she had closely guarded heart's secrets that she revealed only in her diary. She wrote about her mother Santa, who truly cared for her and who was there in times of need.

Her mother had been her anchor ever since her father, her rock and the love of her young life, had died four years earlier.

At the beginning of 2001, in Grade 9 at the Hercules high school in Pretoria West, Alta met a new boy. Jaco was from Birchley in Kempton Park and was in Grade 11. Jaco had an open face and he, too, was blond-haired and blue-eyed. He had a way about him that young girls often admired, a devil-may-care attitude. It bordered on arrogance. He called it his kick-ass attitude.

That personality trait was irresistible to Alta.

Alta, too, had a manner that Jaco noticed and liked. She could be equally self-willed, even manipulative when it came to getting her own way. She called her method "mindfucking", a surprisingly crude word for a girl of only sixteen. Still, she was proud of it and in her diary she once described the result of a confrontation with some people, "I mindfucked them and guess who won?"

The two teenagers, Alta and Jaco, were drawn to each other as if they were magnets. They fell deeply in love. Alta wrote in her diary about how happy she was when she was with Jaco and how much she loved him.

She called him "Adam" in her diary. His nickname for her was "Eve". In their young heads and in their juvenile love, they were the original paradisiacal pair.

To confirm their love for one another, Jaco (17) had a large cross and the immortal names Adam and Eve tattooed on his chest. In that manner, the two beautiful teenagers with the angelic, innocent blue eyes tied their love knot.

It surprised no-one later that they had found each other. Their deep mutual attraction and its horrific consequences was later ascribed to the fact that Adam and Eve, with their special circumstances, found the warmth and security within each other that they had not found elsewhere. This bore within itself the seeds of their crime. For Eve, Adam was a man who desired and protected her and who with her limited insight assumed the role of a father figure. For Adam with his macho manner, Eve was a kind of trophy after whom all the boys hankered. It made him very possessive of her.

Then an intruder appeared who threatened their great love.

In the close togetherness of their romance, both their passion and the demons that had lurked in each of them for so long found expression. It was revealed that Alta and Jaco were anything but innocent, lovesick teenagers. In fact, they were two deeply confused children, the product of dysfunctional families and a living indictment of schools that did not intervene timeously and capably.

Adam and Eve horrifically murdered Alta's mother, the mother about whom Alta had written in her diary, "She does so much for me and I don't know how to repay her."

> **Then an intruder appeared who threatened their great love.**

The widowed mother

The 47-year-old Santa Pretorius had been widowed for four years. She worked hard to keep her head above water, although it was only she and Alta. Her heart was deeply troubled and filled with guilt. As a young bride, she had had great dreams. Like all brides, she had wanted a good husband and a happy family, and beautiful children who would excel and make a parent proud.

She was 24 when Natasha was born. Then already there were problems: drink and quarrels, and more drink. Her husband, the breadwinner, lost his job and the family moved away to attempt a new life. A nomadic life with a drunken father brought greater and more heartrending problems: Natasha was placed in foster care and it left an emotionally weak Santa shattered.

At 31, she fell pregnant again. Little Alta Willene brought hope, but not for long. The same tale of drinking and life on the move followed. Over the course of ten years, Alta attended eight schools. However, in contrast to her mother, Alta could see things through. She did not fail a single year. She was even made prefect and later class captain. Her love for her father did not waver. She ignored his alcohol abuse.

Santa Pretorius

Rapport

Then, in 1997, he lost his battle with his inner demons and committed suicide. Her father's death devastated Alta and she blamed her mother for the suicide.

Santa consoled her twelve-year-old daughter, supported her and tried to bolster her confidence. It is a tremendous blow for any child to lose a parent at such an early age, no matter how imperfect the parent.

Santa thought her love and support were enough, until she unexpectedly found that Alta was smoking dagga. She pleaded and threatened, and told Alta that she would give her away as she had given Natasha away unless Alta gave up her bad habits. Alta took fright and things improved.

In 1998, Santa and Alta moved to Pretoria West where they were closer to her family. She enrolled Alta in a school in Hercules and in the mornings travelled by bus to the hospital in Moot where she worked as a nurse. She worked long hours and Alta was home alone in the afternoons. Alta met the new boyfriend, Jaco Steijn, in Hercules.

Jaco was the sort of influence Santa did not want in her daughter's life. However, the youngsters' love knew no bounds. Santa watched helplessly as Jaco dragged Alta into the abyss with him; with the dagga, Jaco brought harder drugs.

Something had to give, and it did when Alta and Jaco ran away at the beginning of 2001, shortly after the start of their relationship. When they were found, they were detained in the Tutela youth centre in Pretoria North. It was a shelter for youngsters who had lost their way in life. They were evaluated and it was concluded that the two teenagers of sixteen and seventeen seriously needed help to combat their addiction to drink and drugs.

The handsome gardens and peaceful façade of Castle Carey in Pretoria's Nina Park reminded one more of an expensive guesthouse than a rehabilitation clinic. In April 2001, Alta was admitted to the Lapalane unit of Castle Carey, where young drug addicts were treated. There children gained new hope. They were equipped to meet their problems head-on and to escape from the despair and misery of drugs.

Jaco was admitted to a similar centre in Cullinan outside Pretoria. Magaliesoord was also a halfway house, but for young awaiting-trial prisoners. That was not a good sign.

Santa regularly visited her daughter in Castle Carey. She saw the progress and there was new hope in her heart. Santa and Alta sat chatting in the garden. She even had permission to take Alta out and once again, she tried to be an anchor to her. It seemed to be going well and Alta even wrote in her diary about the help and understanding that she was getting from her mother. Alta seemed to react really positively to the treatment. It appeared as if she had won her battle with drugs, and in June, she was ready to be discharged.

For the umpteenth time, Santa decided on a new beginning for her and her daughter. She rented a flat in Gezina and the two moved into flat number 105 in a building called Ontario in Adcock Street. After the July holidays, Alta would be returning to school and with a bit of luck things would work out.

Then Alta came home with the news that Santa had feared: Jaco had been released from Magaliesoord and they were together

> **It seemed to be going well and Alta even wrote in her diary about the help and understanding that she was getting from her mother.**

again. Alta even asked, to the complete dismay of Santa, whether Jaco could move in with them for the time being.

Santa opposed that violently. She pleaded once more with Alta and insisted that her daughter leave Jaco. She said he was bad news and he would ruin her.

But Alta refused to budge; she and Jaco loved each other.

Santa rightly feared that she was losing her daughter again.

However, as much as Alta needed Santa, the mother also depended on her daughter. The daughter had a strong personality and she was almost a crutch for her mother's emotional frailties.

On Friday, 6 July 2001, Alta Oehley saw her sister Santa for the last time. Santa was unhappy because Jaco had returned and it seemed that the dagga had returned with him. All the months of rehabilitation and hope had been in vain. Again, he had brought not only dagga but LSD and Ecstasy, even heroin.

One ... two ... three ...

On Saturday, 7 July 2001, Alta and Jaco took heroin.

Santa noticed it. As a mother and particularly as a mother of a daughter with Alta's history, her radar was finely attuned to Alta's behaviour, appearance and actions. She wanted to talk to Alta but the opportunities were few as Jaco was in the flat all the time.

In the evening, Santa called Alta to her room. She told her that in the future she and Jaco would be allowed to see each other only on Friday evenings.

That really got Alta on her high horse, and mother and daughter had a furious row. Later that evening, Alta reconsidered. She apologised to her mother for her behaviour, saying she was sorry about the row and for her backchatting. From the kitchen, where Alta and Jaco were busy, Alta called out to her mother in front of the TV that she loved her.

However, Santa was upset about the row and about Jaco's hold over her daughter, and she did not react to her daughter's apology.

After supper they sat in the lounge watching TV, all three of them on the sofa with Alta in the middle.

When Santa dozed off, Alta and Jaco could not keep their hands off each other. They got up and crept into the kitchen where they grappled feverishly. Santa heard the scuffling in the kitchen and called out to them. The two, frustrated by the interruption, returned to the lounge and sat down again next to Santa on the sofa in front of the TV.

Santa eventually fell asleep in front of the TV. It was not just a TV snooze but a much deeper sleep. They left her like that and started getting amorous again, the heroin inflaming their brains.

At about two that Sunday morning, Jaco suddenly said, "Let's kill her."

Alta jumped up, fetched a knife from the kitchen and handed it to Jaco.

They crouched over the sleeping mother.

"Count to three," said Jaco.

They counted together, like children playing a game: one . . . two . . . three . . . Jaco started stabbing at the sleeping Santa, Alta egging him on.

Santa started out of her sleep from the stabs. She realised what was happening. She knew about the demons that had taken possession of the children. She struggled and pleaded for her life. They slid off the sofa and landed on the floor. She tried to hide, fending off the knife blows with her arms.

The neighbour heard Santa's hysterical pleas through the thin walls of the flat. "Stop . . . you're hurting me . . . you are going to kill me!" she screamed.

Alta rushed to the kitchen and returned with another knife, determined to silence her mother. She too started stabbing. They stabbed Santa where she lay on the floor.

Jaco used such force that the handle of his steak knife broke off.

Jaco used such force that the handle of his steak knife broke off.

Alta went into the kitchen for a third time to fetch a knife.

They stabbed Santa more than twenty times before her body finally went still and slack. Jaco and Alta stabbed her helpless mother in the neck, face, back, chest and hips, and in her arms when she tried to fend off the knife.

When she was still, Jaco took a shoelace and tied it around Santa's neck. He pulled it tight and choked her to make sure that she was dead.

Santa's blood was smeared all over the two children and on the floor.

Exhausted they sank onto the sofa, smoked a joint, made coffee and drank it with their bloodied hands cupped around the mugs. Then they stepped out into the cold winter's night for fresh air.

Returning after their walk, they avoided the body and got into a bath together to wash off the blood. Then they ate green jelly from the fridge and crawled into bed. After having sex, they made a lovers' pact: they swore they would never part and would always love one another. Then they fell asleep.

Sunday morning they slept late, tired from their nocturnal doings. When they finally got up, they had another bath. In the lounge, they saw their devilish handiwork; saw Santa lying on the lounge floor. They saw the wounds to her body and that some of her clothing had been ripped off in the desperate struggle. And they saw all the dried blood: on the body, the sofa, and especially on the floor. The shoelace was still knotted tightly around her neck.

The two children were unsure of the next step and wondered what to do. The blood could be wiped away and the floor washed, but what to do with the body?

The two children were unsure of the next step and wondered what to do. The blood could be wiped away and the floor washed, but what to do with the body?

Jaco had a plan. He wanted to cut Santa into small pieces and flush her down the toilet. Alta hesitated. It did not sound right, but Jaco convinced her.

However, it was not just a simple matter of cutting; getting through the bones would require a saw.

Later that day they went to the house of Jaco's mother in Pretoria North. There they would find a saw and bigger and sharper butcher's knives. Jaco told his mother they wanted to borrow them for cutting up meat.

With the saw and knives in hand, they crept back into the flat and to the body on the floor.

Jaco looked at the woman on the floor and put down the saw. He could not do it. He told Alta he did not feel like doing it at that moment. It was hard work and he just felt too tired.

They decided to go to Sunnyside where there were drugs and people. There, amid the hustle and bustle, they could escape from the body in the flat. Perhaps when they got back it would be gone.

From where she lay, it would have been easy for someone to see the woman and the blood through the lounge window. They pulled a duvet from a bed and covered Santa with it. Then they dragged her behind the sofa where she could not be seen from the window. They spread blankets over the blood on the floor.

They spent the night drugging in Sunnyside.

On Monday morning, Natasha Marimuthoo (23) received a telephone call from the hospital in the Moot. Natasha was Santa's first daughter who had been fostered but had then been reunited with her mother. The hospital wanted to know where Santa was. She had not arrived at work and there was no reply from her telephone at the flat.

Natasha also phoned the flat, as did Alta Oehley, Santa's sister. They found it strange that Santa had simply stayed away from work. It was completely unlike her. Santa was conscientious and she would walk kilometres to work if she had to.

> **They found it strange that Santa had simply stayed away from work. It was completely unlike her. Santa was conscientious and she would walk kilometres to work if she had to.**

They drove to the flat, which they found locked and deserted. They saw nothing amiss through the windows. They asked Alfred Jonker, the caretaker, to unlock the door. He said the rules did not allow him to do that.

Natasha then phoned the Moot police and reported her mother as missing. However, the police said they had to wait some time before they could start an investigation. Perhaps she was not missing and had merely gone away with someone.

Later that Monday, Alta and Jaco returned to the flat from Sunnyside. They avoided the lounge and carried the microwave to the bedroom to prepare food. They had macaroni and other food, drank, smoked dagga and had sex, as if they had no care in the world.

By Tuesday, Santa had still not reported for work. Natasha phoned the flat again. Alta answered and said her mother had left on Sunday with a strange man in a red Golf and she had not yet returned.

About eleven that morning, Alta started writing in her diary.

The next morning, 11 July, Jaco said he knew where to get a pistol. He was not going to be locked up again as he had been in Tutela and Magaliesoord. Jaco stole the pistol and bullets from a cupboard in a friend's house in Claremont.

They returned to the flat and tried to enter through a window in order to avoid inquisitive eyes. However, the caretaker spotted them and they fled.

He told Santa's family about the two children's strange behaviour and they phoned the police again.

On Thursday, the police and fire brigade arrived at the flat and the caretaker unlocked the door. The flat was in chaos and the smell overwhelming. They found the half-naked, mutilated and putrefying body of Santa under the duvet behind the sofa.

They also found dagga, a saw, a knife blade with the handle broken off, and other knives covered in blood. There were bloody fingerprints on a coffee mug, stale macaroni on the bed, remains of food in glass bowls, and Santa's spectacles with bloodied lenses.

The kitchen was full of unwashed dishes. Clearly, people had been living, eating and sleeping in the flat – with the body.

Everyone, including the policemen, was shocked by the ferocity of the attack on the woman and speculated about the saw. They suspected Satanism as it could only be the work of the devil.

Natasha was hysterical when she identified her mother's body. "They [the murderers] must be punished for ever. My mother was so loving and kind to everyone."

They also found Alta's diaries and a letter in one of the diaries. Natasha recognised Alta's handwriting in the letter. The letter, written in English, was littered with errors:

10 July 2001: 10:59
Right now, we (me & Jaco) are waiting for my uncle to arrive here at the flat where my mom's body is lying. We just moved her so nobody can see her when they are looking through the window.

Adam: Present: My heart is beating like a drum at all the excitement that's happening around us. My girlfriend's uncle is on the way to the flats of Ontario. Where moments ago (me & Alta) moved the furniture to hide the old lady so that if her uncle arrives heal [sic] only see furniture and me & Eve will be in one room full of sadness and paranoia.

* You see we are not bad people, we really do love each other. I'm not going to give in. I'll stand by my man. This Adrenillin [sic] rush was not good for my heart. I know my Baby's also scarred [sic], he just sits there full of stress and mixed emotions. I really didn't want anything bad as this happening. I'm also in my fuckyou in if they catch us today. I'll go on loving my true love and also waiting for him. God I think my uncle is here, please help us.

The police now knew whom to look for.

The trial

On the Thursday afternoon, while the police were making their gruesome discovery at number 105 Ontario, Jaco and Alta were hitchhiking to friends of Jaco's in Kempton Park.

On the way, they sat on a kerb in Hercules and every now and then lifted a thumb. William Harmsen saw the two teenagers from his Golf and stopped to ask if he could give them a lift.

They accepted gratefully. Alta sat in the front and Jaco in the back. Suddenly Jaco pressed the muzzle of the pistol against the back of William's neck.

William pleaded with Jaco not to shoot, saying he had a young child. They told him to stop because they needed his car and money. However, he kept on driving and pleading. Alta pulled the handbrake up hard and the Golf came to a halt.

William pulled out the keys and jumped out. He ran to the nearest house, from where he phoned the police on his cellphone. He saw the two run away from the Golf and he gave chase while still giving the police directions on his phone.

The police were there within minutes. They arrested the two fugitive teenagers that afternoon at about half past four.

Captain Riette Everton of the police occultism unit questioned Alta and Jaco in the Moot police station. Both made complete confessions. They denied ever having been seriously involved in Satanism, although Alta had played with an Ouija board, burnt a Bible and laughed at ministers.

They admitted, though, that they were addicted to drugs.

On Friday, 14 July, in a brief court appearance, they were charged with murder, theft, robbery with aggravating circumstances, and the possession of an unlicensed firearm and ammunition. They were remanded in the cells at the Moot police station.

The twosome appeared in court on 20 July. No relative was willing to post their bail. The control prosecutor of the Pretoria regional court, Madelein Combrink, said it seemed that Jaco's wards did not want him released into their care. Both Alta's parents were dead. "It seems that no-one is prepared to post their bail and neither of the children has a fixed address," Combrink said. The court papers simply noted that Jaco was from Pretoria Gardens and Alta from Gezina.

Alta was taken to a place of safety and Jaco was held in the juvenile section of the Pretoria Local Prison.

When they next appeared in court in September 2001, Alta and Jaco embraced each other and blew kisses during the proceedings. Jaco's stepfather and Alta's aunt were in court as their wards, but still no bail had been posted.

Afterwards, Alta wept heartbreakingly as Jaco was taken away, back to the courtroom cells.

Their trial in the Pretoria High Court started in May 2002. The exhibits in court included love letters, a saw and a knife.

The proceedings took place in camera and the accused were referred to as "Adam" and "Eve" to protect their identities as minors. They pleaded guilty to all charges.

A psychiatric evaluation found that Alta had narcissistic tendencies and that she was manipulative and impulsive. She said her mother never cared for her and was insensitive to her needs.

Jaco's behavioural problems caused tension in his relationship with his mother. Although his father was mostly absent during his childhood, he hero-worshipped him.

Criminologist Dr Irma Labuschagne testified that if the death sentence had still been in force it would have been an appropriate punishment for the two "evil" teenagers. Their behaviour was the result of a long process. Both were also masters of manipulation, especially because they seemed so innocent.

Alta said she never received love from her mother. When she was small, her mother had once wanted to scald her with a frying pan for not wanting to eat her food. Alta had tired of her mother's nagging demands and orders.

Her mother had also threatened Alta when she was little that she would give her away, just as she had done with her other sister. "Every day I was scared that it would happen."

Alta told of their nomadic lifestyle and of her alcoholic father.

Jaco, too, had a disrupted childhood. He was the middle child of three and his parents divorced when he was three. For two years, his mother and the three children struggled to survive financially. Jaco told Dr Labuschagne about his mother's neglect of him and his sister because she had to work double shifts to earn money.

"My parents were interested in absolutely nothing about me: not in my achievements, nothing, not even a rugby match."

In Grade 2, Jaco stole R50 and was placed in the school hostel for his behavioural problems. In Grade 3, at another primary school, he became involved in Satanism.

In the meantime, his mother remarried and in the same year she placed Jaco in yet another primary school. There, in Grade 3, he stole a bicycle and in Grade 4 sweets that he gave to his sister.

He started high school at the Pretoria Gardens Technical School and started smoking dagga. In Grade 9, he was expelled from school for aggressive behaviour.

Next, Jaco was sent to high school in Middelburg in Mpumalanga, where he was expelled from the hostel. He then started using LSD and Ecstasy.

> **"My parents were interested in absolutely nothing about me: not in my achievements, nothing, not even a rugby match."**

After that, he went to stay with his father and new stepmother. His father registered him at the D F Malan high school, from which he was expelled yet again. In the Birchley high school, he started smoking rocks and using heroin.

He left there too and finally ended up in the Hercules high school in Pretoria West, where he met Alta.

Dr Labuschagne testified that Jaco typified antisocial behaviour. Both she and Acting Justice Lizette Meyer were of the opinion that Jaco had become a victim of "the system" early in life.

As to why they killed Santa, Jaco told Dr Labuschagne, "I think it was because she and other people pressured us too much emotionally. I wanted to protect my girlfriend. I felt Alta's mother was driving us to it [murder]. And not just her, everyone. We have both had difficult childhoods."

While he was an awaiting-trial prisoner, Jaco joined a prison gang and had the gang's name, the 26s, tattooed on him.

On Sunday, 15 July, a week after her mother's murder and while in custody, Alta wrote about her feelings and the events.

"Heart: empty as a drum", she started.

After Jaco began stabbing her mother, "I sat on the sofa, watching. Then I walked to the kitchen to fetch myself a knife. I came back and started stabbing her. I felt like a zombie.

"Afterwards we went to have a bath. I started to faint, I don't know why.

"On 9 July [Sunday] we were back in the flat [after fetching the saw]. He and I spent about the whole day in the bedroom, because the body and all the blood gave us the shivers."

Ms Justice Meyer sentenced each to twenty years in prison. She ordered Alta to serve at least fifteen years and to receive rehabilitation before becoming eligible for parole.

The judge said it was clear from Alta's diaries that she and Jaco had led a life of unbridled sex, drugs and alcohol before the murder, with no respect for authority.

Although Jaco was older, it was clear that Alta was more intelligent and that she had manipulated him with sex.

The judge found that drugs had probably been the main reason for the murder. Regarding the plan to dismember the body and flush it down the toilet, she said, "They clearly did not have the stomach for it. They simply did not know what to do with the body."

She said the tragedy could have been avoided if Jaco had had proper treatment earlier. However, not one of the schools that expelled him had intervened.

Natasha, who initially wanted her younger sister to be punished "for ever" for murdering their mother, hugged Alta tightly after the sentencing. Both wept.

Alta's legal counsel said about that moment, "It was astonishing. They grew up separately and there was no bond between them. This event [the murder of their mother] has brought them together."

Santa's family described Alta as a rebel, while her father's family called her a peacemaker.

Alta took a photograph with her to jail. It was of herself and her mother sitting together on a step – just like any other happy mother and daughter.

A deadly duo

As the flowers are all made sweeter
by the sunshine and the dew,
So this old world is made brighter
by the lives of folks like you.

A visitor reading this sensitive verse on a headstone in Texas might wonder what had made the occupant of the grave so special to warrant such words of dedication: Bonnie Parker, born 1 October 1910, died 23 May 1934. What did this young woman do during her fleeting 24 years on earth to be lauded like this?

The visitor would have to look further afield for an answer. He would have to look to the headstone of another Texan grave, that of Clyde Chestnut Barrow. He was only 25 when he died on that selfsame day, 23 May 1934.

Then one would have to retrace the steps of Bonnie and Clyde to the Great Depression of the early thirties, to unemployment, hardship, famine, to banks repossessing homes and turning families out onto the street to perish wretchedly.

The saga of Bonnie and Clyde was born in that time. It enthralled the entire United States: the two young people who challenged the system blamed for all the misery and penury. Bonnie and Clyde robbed and shot, and the poor of the land worshipped them. While the police were hunting them all over Texas, Oklahoma, Missouri, Louisiana and New Mexico, they were even romantically described as Romeo and Juliet reborn, as a Robin Hood couple who robbed the rich.

On their raids, they took many photographs of each other, as any amorous couple would. Bonnie wrote long poems: *Suicide Sal* and *The Street Girl*. Her last, *The Trail's End*, she wrote shortly before the two ran into a police ambush in their stolen Ford V8 on a lonely dirt road near Bienville Parish in Louisiana on 23 May 1934.

The couple died in a hail of 130 police bullets without an opportunity to surrender. Roughly 20 000 people attended Bonnie's funeral. Her mother put the inscription on her daughter's grave.

Almost 50 years later, South Africa had its own Bonnie and Clyde. However, they did not only rob, they also murdered. And for them there were no tributes.

The meeting

It was not a happy home; money was always in short supply. But curiously, whenever things turned really desperate there was always stronger stuff than water to drink.

Leo Phillips – his friends called him Hoppy – was an electrician and his wife Magdalene Bernadette was pregnant, once again. She complained bitterly because it was already tough at home with three little ones. Now another was on the way. However, the raucous boozing carried on, with never a thought for tomorrow's cares. By the time Mr and Mrs Phillips's seventh baby was born, the father was a psychopath and a hardened pothead, the mother an alcoholic and later a prostitute.

Such were the dismal circumstances into which the fourth baby, Charmaine Helen, was born on 22 July in the winter of 1963.

A report by the social worker, Mrs L Syfrets, later revealed that little Charmaine had been denied a fair start in life in that home.

When she was eight years old and by then familiar with drunkenness and violent domestic quarrels, her mother tried to murder Hoppy. The welfare service investigated the home and removed Charmaine from her parents' care. They placed her in a children's home. Some of the other children were also taken away.

In the children's home, Charmaine was often beaten, mostly for wetting her bed at night. She was punished but no-one ever bothered to determine the causes.

> **A report by the social worker, Mrs L Syfrets, later revealed that little Charmaine had been denied a fair start in life in that home.**

She was twelve years old when both parents were admitted to institutions, respectively for the rehabilitation of alcoholics and for psychotherapeutic treatment. The two finally divorced in 1971.

In 1975, Mrs Phillips was discharged from the Town Hill hospital in Pietermaritzburg. Her drinking problem was under control. Her children, including Charmaine, were returned to her.

Life was extremely tough because reliance on Hoppy and his financial contributions was hardly an option. His dagga use put him at odds with the law. Mrs Phillips, a mother of seven, became a prostitute.

The welfare service removed the children once again and placed them in foster care.

Charmaine later received the shocking although not altogether unexpected news that her mother had been beaten to death in a drunken brawl.

She ran away from foster care and joined the ranks of Durban's street children. At fourteen, she too became a prostitute.

The police arrested her for drug possession and released her into the care of her father Hoppy, who was working in Vryheid repairing fridges.

However, Charmaine saw no bright future for herself with her father and his new wife Nicolene. Hoppy could not manage his daughter anyway and she ended up in a trade school for problem children.

The trade school could not contain her either and she ran away to Port Elizabeth. There she met a Greek sailor in one of the many pubs for mariners from all corners of the earth. At fifteen, Charmaine had a criminal history in Durban and was pregnant to boot. She married Gavnil Skubides, who promised to fetch her and the baby on his next voyage and take them to Greece. There, all would be moonshine and roses. His ship left and Charmaine gave birth to Ricky-Lee. Due to her youth and desperate personal circumstances, the infant boy was immediately taken from her and put up for adoption.

She hoped that hubby Skubides would return and that they would be able to persuade the welfare service that they were happy parents who wanted their child back.

Charmaine waited and waited, but she was impatient and Port Elizabeth was not such an enticing place any longer. When Mr Skubides's ship tied up in the port again and he walked ashore to take his bride and Ricky-Lee to Greece, there was no trace of them.

At seventeen, she was back with her father and revisiting her old haunts in Durban.

By December 1981, Charmaine was a hardened drinker. She was well acquainted with dagga and men from an early age, and she wondered what Christmas had in store for her.

Then Dad Hoppy had a request: could she help him out with a supply of weed for the quiet days over Christmas? She was sure she could help her old man with a finger or two, because she knew many people.

Peter David was the youngest of Pieter and Siena Grundlingh's three sons. Young Peter − or simply Piet or Boeta − was the apple of his mother's eye. He was a quiet and home-loving boy who liked to help his mother with chores in and around the house. He boxed and played rugby at the Vorentoe high school in Brixton in Johannesburg, but he did not really have friends. Peter preferred to keep busy at home.

The Grundlinghs were not prosperous, but the parents tried to provide their sons with a good education and to teach them solid values. Adam was the eldest, followed by Theuns and Peter.

The Grundlinghs were not prosperous, but the parents tried to provide their sons with a good education and to teach them solid values.

Peter was devoted to his father and they often went to watch sports events, especially rugby matches, at Peter's school. In Standard 9 (Grade 11), the year before he matriculated, Peter's peaceful home life was shattered by his father's death from a heart attack.

When he announced soon afterwards that he was leaving school because he wanted to work like his two elder brothers, his mother was not particularly pleased with his decision. However, she let him be. He started an apprenticeship with an electrician and later qualified as a boilermaker.

His mother and brothers knew Peter to be hard-working and conscientious. He had learnt good values at home and they expected good things from him in the future. One thing he had learnt, and which particularly Adam had drilled into him, was that you always admitted your mistakes and tried to fix them. You never walked away from them because they always caught up with you.

His newly gained freedom from school also brought new friends. But some of them had not learnt all those values and insights in their parental homes. Peter was vulnerable to influences and enjoyed having good mates for the first time.

However, they were not as good as he had thought. His mother and brothers were deeply shocked one day when the police arrived with a warrant of arrest for Peter.

He was sentenced to two years for car theft.

In prison, the friends were not top-notch either. Peter developed a rebellious streak and had his body tattooed with blue images of daggers and chains, a horse's head and a naked woman. He was one of the boys.

After his release, he spoke little and drank much. He also met Yvonne Shaw. They got married and named their first-born Martin, after Peter's brother Theuns, christened Marthinus. The union did not last, though, and after two years, Peter and Yvonne divorced. She gained custody of little Martin.

Peter, on the loose again, heard about lots of work at Richards Bay where large coal terminals were under construction. It was also far away from Johannesburg and its associated misery. He hit the road. Dagga and stronger drugs now amplified his drinking.

Peter was not averse to either dagga or blondes and went along on the drive to Durban.

In Richards Bay, Peter met a chap who quizzed him about dagga and who said he knew a beautiful blonde-haired girl to whom he wanted to introduce Peter. As a bachelor, Peter was not averse to either dagga or blondes and went along on the drive to Durban.

On 24 December 1981, Peter Grundlingh (34) was introduced to eighteen-year-old Charmaine Phillips. They had been brought together by a request for dagga from Charmaine's father.

It was a fatal encounter.

Bonnie and Clyde

Peter and Charmaine soon discovered they spoke the same language and they fell in love. He took her to Johannesburg to meet his mother and brothers. She also met Martin, Peter's son from his first marriage.

Peter became obsessively jealous of Charmaine. He forced her to tattoo his name on her stomach. That was how he branded her as his property and tried to keep other men's hands off her.

Four months after their first meeting in April 1982, she fell pregnant and Peter became even more possessive. He burnt her clothes and instructed her to wear clothes bought only by him. He left his work in Richards Bay and they moved to Johannesburg for the birth of their child. Peter was hoping for a girl because he already had a boy.

With the birth of baby Pietertjie in December 1982, Peter was furious about having another son and he even assaulted Charmaine. Having seen the flipside of her lover, she decided not to go through that kind of family life again; her own had been bad enough. In the New Year, she tried to leave him but he fetched her back and threatened her.

In the meantime, the police were on his trail for firearm theft. He was arrested but his mother posted bail to get him out of the cells.

He had to stand trial in the Krugersdorp magistrate's court in June 1983.

That May, Charmaine could stand the assaults on her no longer and she fled with Pietertjie to her brother Robert in Vryheid. Robert was shocked to see her: an eye was swollen shut, her lips were split, her face was bruised, and her body and legs were beaten black and blue.

Three days later Peter was in Vryheid too. He threatened to shoot everyone – Charmaine and Pietertjie, and Charmaine's brother and sister-in-law – unless his wife returned to him.

Charmaine relented and she and Pietertjie left Vryheid with Peter. They headed for Durban. That night they slept on the beachfront in the car, a blue Cortina. They hardly had money for food and Pietertjie cried with hunger.

The next day, Peter and Charmaine pawned the baby carriage and some of their clothing. With a few rands in their pocket, they went looking for dagga and liquor, and some milk for Pietertjie's bottle. In Point Road they stopped at an old haunt of Peter's, a sleazy bar full of shady characters. Charmaine and the baby waited in the car.

Peter popped inside for a drink. He had a few and met Jerry. Soon the two were knocking them back like long-lost pals. Jerry had dagga but it was not for sale. He was prepared to share it, though, if they smoked it together. Jerry left his car behind and climbed in with Peter and Charmaine, and with the wailing Pietertjie.

In the car, Jerry lapsed into boozy lewdness and Charmaine looked enticing in her short dress. His hand started to wander and it landed on her thigh.

She furiously slapped his hand away and snapped at him. Did he think that she was a loose woman whom he could just fondle? The last time a man could just grab her was after he had paid. Her prostitute days were long gone. She did not want to think or be reminded of them. Now she was the mother of Pietertjie, there with them in the car.

Peter was furious too and he scowled. He could not stand it when other men looked at Charmaine. She was his and his name was tattooed on her body. He turned away from the sea and headed towards Stanger. He stopped at a sugar plantation, where he and Jerry got out and lit their dagga joints. Charmaine got out too and smoked with them. Then Pietertjie, barely seven months old and starving, started crying.

"We must get some milk for Pietertjie," she said to the smoking men and got back into the car.

> **He could not stand it when other men looked at Charmaine. She was his and his name was tattooed on her body.**

Suddenly a shot rang out and Jerry fell down. Peter crouched down and looked for money in Jerry's pockets. He got back into the car.

It was Wednesday, 15 June 1983, and the first victim of Peter and Charmaine lay dead: Gerald Douglas Meyer (34).

They drove back to Durban where they tried to set Jerry's car alight. Then they took off for Richards Bay. There Peter also knew places where drink and dagga could be had, and in a hotel he ran into an old friend from his pre-Charmaine days. The friend was smitten with Charmaine and he invited them to sleep over in his house. They stayed for three days.

On Saturday, Peter turned up at the house with a case of beer and an unknown friend, Vernon. Charmaine missed her brother Robert in Vryheid and suggested they go there. Peter invited Vernon along. Vernon said he had nothing special to do and had actually wanted to go to Empangeni. However, he would come with them for the ride and pay for the petrol. They left on Sunday morning, but when Peter stopped at a filling station Vernon said he had no money.

At Melmoth, Pietertjie wailed non-stop again. His bottle was empty. Charmaine asked Peter and Vernon to buy milk and something for her to eat.

They returned with liquor from a shebeen. Charmaine was furious. They set off and outside Melmoth Peter pulled off the road among some trees, where they relieved themselves of all the liquid.

Suddenly, Peter pulled out the firearm and they tied Vernon to a tree. Vernon realised that things looked bleak for him and he pleaded, saying he would give them money. Charmaine laughed at him, but his pleading and Pietertjie's crying from the car irritated her. Peter shot him, took his wallet and they drove back to the friend's house in Richards Bay.

It was Sunday, 19 June 1983. Vernon Alexander Swart (28), their second victim, slumped dead from the tree trunk.

The papers reported on the bodies that had been found, those of Jerry and Vernon. The calibre of the fatal bullets coincided; they came from the same firearm. Major Danie Huggett from Eshowe, the investigating officer, learnt of a man and woman who had been spotted in the company of both victims: perhaps they could provide leads for tracing the murderer.

Peter read the articles. On Monday, they drove to Durban. They slept cosily in a hotel room paid for with Vernon's money. On Tuesday, they drove north, away from the two murder scenes.

In the meantime, a warrant for Peter's arrest had been issued in Krugersdorp. He had not shown up in court to stand trial on the charge of possessing a stolen firearm. However, the search for him was somewhat listless as many warrants were issued for suspects who did not appear in court. The police had their hands full with criminals such as murderers.

Later that same week the blue Cortina pulled into Ermelo on the Vaal River. Peter and Charmaine felt more at ease. They were far from Durban and the two bodies.

On Saturday, 25 June 1983, Peter left a pub with a new boon companion, as was his wont by now. The new mate was a certain Boet.

Peter missed his mother Siena, already 65 by now, and suggested they drive to Johannesburg to visit her. Boet said it was fine by him; he was in for the trip.

Near Secunda, Peter remembered friends who lived in the town: Tjaart and Maria van Heerden. They found the house and knocked. Although the Van Heerdens were entertaining family to a braai, they reluctantly invited Peter and his entourage – Charmaine, the baby and the stranger Boet – to join the intimate gathering.

Later that afternoon, they watched a rugby match on TV. Boet said he had R400 in the bank and he wanted to bet on the outcome of the game. Peter and Charmaine were flat broke; Vernon's money had not lasted long.

They drank and smoked dagga, and decided they were not welcome any longer. Peter was too drunk to drive, so he and baby Pietertjie lay sleeping on the back seat. Charmaine was at the wheel. Boet was ticking with booze and dope, and Charmaine was pretty.

He became familiar and she took offence. She stopped at the Kinross Dam, pulled out the firearm and ordered the dumbfounded Boet to get out of the car. He was frightened out of his wits and pleaded with her. She demanded his savings book and Help-U-Card with its PIN. He was on his knees in front of her when she pulled the trigger.

Only when she was back in the car and Peter had emerged from his drunken stupor, did Charmaine tell him why Boet was no longer there with them.

The left the body of Barend Eugène (Boet) Greyvenstein, their third victim, next to the dam late that Saturday

> **Only when she was back in the car and Peter had emerged from his drunken stupor, did Charmaine tell him why Boet was no longer there with them.**

afternoon of 25 June 1983, and decided to drive to Bloemfontein to shake off the police.

The police found Boet's body. The bullet that ended his life was the same calibre as those found in the two bodies in Natal. Three murders had been committed with the same weapon.

Captain Ivor Human of Durban's murder and robbery unit ran the investigation. Boet's tracks were retraced. They led from a pub in Ermelo to a braai in Secunda, to a fatal shot at the Kinross Dam. In Secunda, the police obtained names and descriptions.

In Bloemfontein, Peter and Charmaine saw on *Police File* on TV that the police were keen to talk to a Mr Peter Louis David Grundlingh, about 35, with fair hair and tattoos all over his body: chains around his ankles and naked women on his thighs. He was in the company of a young blonde woman and a baby, and they were travelling in a blue Cortina.

Newspapers soon dubbed the fugitive couple Bonnie and Clyde.

On Thursday, 30 June, Peter used Boet's Help-U-Card to draw money at an ATM in Bloemfontein. Another customer, Martin Mofosi, asked Peter to help him draw money as well. Martin also asked them for a lift.

They needed money and Martin had a bank card. They agreed to take him along.

On the way to Dewetsdorp, near the prison at Groenvlei, Peter stopped at a roadside pull-off. Martin got out and urinated next to the car. Charmaine was furious. Peter slapped Martin, who hit back. Charmaine jumped out of the car with the firearm and shot Martin in the head. They took his bank card and drew another R60 from his account.

Martin Mofosi (25), father of five children and husband to Annika, a domestic, was their fourth victim.

They left the Cortina and cadged a ride to Pietermaritzburg, where they stole a white Mazda. They managed to dodge the police for another 14 days. By then Charmaine was deeply worried. She knew about the country-wide police search for them and feared the inevitable outcome.

Peter said he could not face jail again. Charmaine was scared that Pietertjie would be harmed in a final confrontation with the police.

With the stolen Mazda, they drove to Johannesburg and went to ground in a Mayfair hotel room.

On Thursday evening, 14 July, they drove to the home of Peter's eldest brother, Adam, and his wife, Jacoba, who lived in a flat in Loveday Street in Braamfontein. The other brother, Theuns, had gassed himself after his wife had left him; about the same time that Peter and Charmaine met.

Peter and Charmaine were afraid the police were watching the flat. They were in a hurry and when Jacoba opened the door, Charmaine thrust Pietertjie into the astonished Jacoba's arms and the two of them drove to Germiston.

Peter saw an ad in a newspaper for a motorbike for sale. The stolen Mazda was too "hot" and had become a liability by then. He phoned Greg Botes, the owner, and asked whether he could take the motorbike for a test ride the next morning. Greg consented.

On Friday morning, 15 July, Peter and Charmaine turned up in the Mazda at Greg's block of flats, Monte Vista, in Blackheath. The bike was a powerful, red 1 000 cc Kawasaki.

Greg stared at them as they rode off. When they had not returned after a few hours, he phoned the police with a description of the couple and his stolen machine.

At about one o'clock on Friday afternoon, the police received a call from Vereeniging. A woman reported seeing a couple that looked to her like the fugitives Bonnie and Clyde.

Frans de Klerk and Nico Oosthuizen of Vereeniging's murder and robbery unit spotted the red Kawasaki in Grey Avenue. They drove in front of it and forced it off the road. Nico jumped out and grabbed the keys.

A crowd of curious onlookers congregated at the scene. Peter and Charmaine removed their crash helmets when the two policemen started questioning them. Peter said he knew nothing. His surname was De Jager. Charmaine said her name was Dawn.

The detectives arrested them and found the white Mazda later that day. Inside it were nappies, nappy pins, women's clothing, liquor bottles and milk. Fingerprints on the stolen car, registration number NP 79822, corresponded with those of Peter Grundlingh and Charmaine Phillips.

On Friday night, Peter received a special visitor in the charge office of the Brixton murder and robbery unit. The police had allowed Siena, his aged and sickly mother, to greet her favourite son Boeta, the quiet and home-loving one. When mother and son saw each other, they embraced and wept together.

Pietertjie

A week after their 22 July arrest, Charmaine turned twenty. The police escorted her and Peter to Durban for questioning and for their trial in the Pietermaritzburg Supreme Court.

They were indicted on four charges of murder, four of armed robbery, two of fraud and one of theft. The court case started in October 1983. The judge president of Natal (now KwaZulu-Natal), Mr Justice John Milne, presided.

Charmaine appeared in court neatly dressed. With her wavy blonde hair, she was the picture of respectability. Peter, too, was neatly turned out in a jacket and tie.

However, it did not take long for Charmaine's veneer to flake off. She spat at photographers from the dock, threw her wads of chewing gum around, stuck out her tongue and swore at people. "Aw, f . . . you all!" she once screamed loudly. She exclaimed to a policeman escorting her to the court cells, "It's my f . . . life, not yours!"

Various versions were proffered of who did the actual shooting.

The evening after the arrest in Vereeniging, Peter and Charmaine made separate statements.

Peter said he had shot all four men. Charmaine said Peter had shot the first three and she had shot Martin Mofosi.

Peter then testified that his statement was false. He had shot no-one. He had only wanted to protect Charmaine, who had shot all four.

Charmaine testified that while she and Peter were on the run, they had agreed about what they were going to say when they were caught. Peter said he would confess to all four murders because Charmaine was still young and had to care for Pietertjie.

However, she had decided in the meantime to tell the "truth". She had shot the men because they "irritated" her. She proceeded to describe how she had first shot Jerry, then Vernon, then Boet and finally Martin in the head.

Her legal counsel, Advocate Dawie de Villiers, conceded that Charmaine had done the shooting but said there were extenuating circumstances: she had shot Jerry because her baby was crying with hunger.

The judge remarked, "If people had to be shot because babies were crying, this country would be a bloodbath."

Charmaine Phillips and Peter Grundlingh in court

State Advocate John van der Bergh said Charmaine was assuming culpability to save Peter from the gallows. She knew that, thanks to her youth and motherhood, she would not be sentenced to death

> **"If people had to be shot because babies were crying, this country would be a bloodbath."**

Judge Milne convicted them guilty on all charges, except for the armed robbery of Jerry Meyer, their first victim. He said it did not matter who had pulled the trigger because the murders had been committed for a common purpose and they were co-culpable.

He said both accused were unreliable witnesses and Charmaine had not impressed him as a "refined woman that one would find in a Victorian drawing room". The judge accepted as an extenuating circumstance her "very unhappy youth" in which she had had no opportunity of building up sound moral judgment.

He also alluded to Marlene Lehnberg, the notorious scissors murderess, who had been spared the death penalty due to her youth.

On 23 February 1984, Peter's sobbing mother, hunched in a court bench, her frail shoulders bent, heard the judge in a black cap pronounce the death penalty four times over her youngest son. He also sentenced Peter to 36 years in prison on the other charges.

Charmaine received four life sentences, with no prospect of parole.

For almost 18 months, Peter and his legal representatives battled to have the death penalty set aside. In the meantime, his mother's heart simply gave in and she passed away, as did his eldest brother Adam. Of his whole family, only Peter was left, and his hourglass was empty too.

He was notified that he would be hanged on 30 July 1985, a week after Charmaine's 22nd birthday. Four days before his execution, Charmaine was allowed to bid him farewell.

Before being parted forever, Peter swore a solemn oath to Charmaine: he would write a letter in which he would admit to shooting all four men.

The letter, he hoped, would help get Charmaine out of jail.

He also sent a last "public message" to a newspaper for publication. "I have one big advantage over you – I know when I am going to die and I have made my peace with the Old Guy upstairs. You out there do not know when your time is due. Many of you are going to be caught unawares before you would have had the time to get to know Christ."

On Tuesday, 30 July 1985, at seven in the morning, Peter died on the gallows. He died without showing remorse for his four victims and without a last parting thought for his mother, whom he had caused so much sorrow.

In her first six years in prison, Charmaine was practically impossible to contain. She caused chaos and often spent time in solitary confinement for her repeated violations of the rules.

Then she started calming down and in the Kroonstad prison for women she passed Standard 8 (Grade 10), qualified as a hairdresser and turned out to be a gifted artist.

After Charmaine had been in prison for fifteen years, Brigadier Ivor Human, investigating officer at the time of the hunt for Bonnie and Clyde, took her a letter. It was Peter's letter, which he had promised to write shortly before his execution. On the strength of the letter, Charmaine fruitlessly petitioned three state presidents for release. The prison authorities advised her to apply for parole after twenty years on the grounds of good behaviour.

During all her years in prison, Charmaine kept asking after their son, Pietertjie. She longed for him and hoped he would have better moral judgment, the judgment she had never been granted.

But the news about Pietertjie was not encouraging. It seemed that the son who had witnessed four murders as a baby, whose father had died on the gallows, and whose mother was in prison, had also not managed to keep to the straight and narrow.

By the age of four, he already knew what had happened to his parents. At twelve, he ran away from a children's home to a life on the streets of Johannesburg. There he became addicted to crack cocaine.

He led the same nomadic life as his mother when she was a teenager, from foster homes to children's homes, to an underworld of drink, drugs and crime. He landed in jail in Leeukop and in Sun City (Diepkloof outside Johannesburg), and then for nine months in the Kroonstad juvenile prison, close to his mother in the women's prison.

Shortly after midnight on Friday, 20 August 2004, Charmaine, then 40 years old, was released on parole. She had spent twenty years in the Kroonstad prison. The Department of Correctional Services issued a written statement on her behalf in which she begged forgiveness for the murders and for her initial "negative attitude" in prison.

During all her years in prison, Charmaine kept asking after their son, Pietertjie.

Pietertjie (21) moved in with his mother in her Kroonstad flat. However, after a while she was unable to tolerate the situation. They were both subject to parole conditions and Charmaine was afraid that Pietertjie's wild lifestyle and habits would land her back in jail. Ten days before his birthday, his first with his mother, she kicked him out of the flat.

He returned to the streets of Johannesburg.

Charmaine Phillips after her release

In February 2006, Pietertjie admitted to a newspaper that he was HIV positive, that he had Aids and that he had been making a living as a gay prostitute for the past number of years. "The way I see it, I don't have long to live," he said in Vrededorp at the age of 23. When he gave the interview, a front tooth had been knocked out and there was a wound on one arm where a client had bitten him. Under one eye was a black bruise and between his fingers he held his rock pipe for smoking crack cocaine.

Barely a month after that confession, on Sunday morning, 19 March, Pietertjie was found dead in bed in the flatlet of friends of his in the Vrededorp old-age home. He had died of a heroin overdose.

With the permission of correctional services, Charmaine, pale and distraught, attended her child's cremation in the Rand Funerals' chapel in Brixton.

Among the handful of mourners at Pietertjie's memorial service was Martin Grundlingh, Peter's son from his brief marriage to Yvonne. Martin was eight when his father was hanged.

Martin had regularly tried to concern himself with his half-brother Pietertjie and had even visited him two nights before his death.

He said, "He [Pietertjie] talked of dying and of hurting people. But that was the hurt he felt in himself. His bruised soul had taken him down the wrong roads and there were just too many whys and wherefores between him and his mother."

Charmaine returned to her work in a Kroonstad hairdressing salon after Pietertjie's cremation. Another sad chapter in her life story had ended. Without popular adulation or sentimental rhymes as tributes, she was married on Saturday, 21 July 2007, to Hennie Rabie. Afterwards she posed for her wedding photographs dressed in a denim ensemble and black boots. Her blonde hair was cropped short and she smiled shyly.

Other books in Chris Karsten's TRUE CRIME series

Headline murders: Slayings which shook South Africa
Ten real-life tales of murder go beyond mere statistics to the people behind the headlines.

The death of former first lady Marike de Klerk spawned rumours of a political killing and dissension in the family; the story of Casper Greeff, respected dentist and dedicated husband, found guilty of paying to have his lovely wife murdered, is one steeped in envy and intrigue; the Bain's Kloof murder is an unsettling account of how a history of deprivation created human killing machines; and other notorious murder cases that have gripped the public imagination.

Unsolved: No answers to heinous South African crimes
Was the controversial Dutch Reformed theologian Johan Heyns murdered by right-wingers or by his own people? Have the Scorpions made any progress in their search for paedophile Gert van Rooyen's young victims? Have Chris Hani's killers revealed the whole truth? What did Robert Smit know that made it so important to have him silenced? Why have the perpetrators still not been brought to justice?

Ten of South Africa's most baffling crime mysteries are revisited and provide the reader with a sense of the real human tragedies behind these haunting events.

Killer Women: Fatal South African Females
Ten true stories of women driven to kill by passion and sometimes despair.

For the first time, the full story of the tragic death of Oscar winner Charlize Theron's father is told. Also, the Marico, backdrop to the stories of Herman Charles Bosman, hits the headlines again when a grandmother sprinkles rat poison over her lover's sandwiches. Dina Rodrigues hires four men to kill her lover's baby, and the "Baby Jordan" case generates unprecedented publicity.